Nigel Cawthorne is the author of 175 books under his own name and as Al Cimino, Alexander Macdonald, Gordon Bowers and Karl Streisand. He is thought to be the most published living author in the UK. He was called to testify to the US Senate over *The Bamboo Cage*. *The Iron Cage* prompted questions in both houses of the British parliament. *Sex Lives of the US Presidents* got him on the *Joan Rivers Show* and *Sex Lives of the Popes* got him on the biggest chat show in Brazil. He lives in Bloomsbury, London, just a few minutes walk from the British Library where he spends his time writing books.

CW00840847

Other books by Nigel Cawthorne

The Empress of South America – The Irish Courtesan Who Destroyed Paraguay and Became
   Its National Heroine
Flight MH370 – The Mystery
The Bamboo Cage – The True Story of American POWs in Vietnam
The Iron Cage – Are British POWs Still Alive in Siberia?
Daughter of Heaven – The True Story of the Only Woman to Become Emperor of China
Takin' Back My Name – The Confessions of Ike Turner
Reaping the Whirlwind – Voices of the Enemy from World War II
Sex Lives of the Popes
Sex Lives of the US Presidents
Sex Lives of the Great Dictators
Sex Lives of the Kings and Queens of England
Sex Lives of the Hollywood Goddesses
Sex Lives of the Hollywood Idols
Sex Lives of the Great Artists
Sex Lives of the Great Composers
Sex Lives of the Hollywood Goddesses 2
Sex Lives of the Famous Gays
Sex Lives of the Famous Lesbians
Sex Lives of the Roman Emperors
Strange Laws of Old England
Curious Cures of Old England
Amorous Antics of Old England
Sex Secrets of Old England
Beastly Battles of Old England
Flight MH370: The Mystery
Vietnam: A War Lost and Won
House of Horrors: The True Story of Josef Fritzl, The Father from Hell
Jack the Ripper's Secret Confession
Jeremy Clarkson: Motormouth
Magical Mythtery Tour
The History of the SS Cricket Team
The Alien Who Thought He Was Elvis
Che Guevara – The Last Conquistador
Julius Caesar
Alexander the Great
Blond Ambition: The Rise and Rise of Boris Johnson
David Cameron – Class Act
Alan Johnson – Left Standing
Jeremy Corbyn – Leading from the Left
Portraits of Power
Ian Fleming: Licence to Kill
Harry – A Prince Among Men
A Bit of Stephen Fry

Taking Charge
The Biography of Theresa May

Nigel Cawthorne

First published by Endeavour Press Ltd in 2016.

www.nigelcawthorne.com

Table of Contents

Chapter One – Queen of the May

It was a coronation – and one undertaken as breakneck speed. While it was a full four months between the death of George VI in February 1952 and Elizabeth II's coronation that June, not even four weeks had passed since David Cameron had fallen on his sword following his defeat in the EU referendum on 24 June 2016 when the chairman of the 1922 Committee of backbench Conservative MPs, Graham Brady, announced on 12 July that Theresa May had been "elected" the new leader of the Conservative Party with immediate effect. David Cameron would then hold one last cabinet meeting the following day. He would then take his final Prime Minister's Question the following day. Afterwards he would go to Buckingham Palace to give his resignation to the Queen. Her Majesty's next visitor would be Mrs May, who was then formerly anointed as PM. The Russian newspapers were already asking whether she was "the new Iron Lady", while Fox News in the US and the *Yorkshire Post* were also comparing her to Margaret Thatcher.

There are some similarities between Britain's two woman Prime Ministers. Both were from a relatively humble background. While Mrs Thatcher was the daughter of a grocer and Methodist preacher in Grantham, Lincolnshire, Mrs May is the daughter of a Church of England clergyman and was brought up in similarly rural Oxfordshire.

While Margaret Thatcher was fifty-three when she took office, Theresa Mary was fifty-nine. She was born on 1 October 1956 in Eastbourne where her thirty-nine-year-old father Hubert Brasier was chaplain at All Saint's Hospital. Her mother, Zaidee Mary Brasier, née Barnes, was twenty-eight when she gave birth to her only child. Both Theresa's grandmothers had been in domestic service and her great-grandfather had been a butler born in a Scottish mining village.

The family moved to Oxfordshire when Hubert became vicar of Enstone and Heyrope, near Chipping Norton, later home to David Cameron, Jeremy Clarkson, Rebekah Brooks of News International and others of the influential Chipping Norton set. But then the Braisers had moved eighteen miles across the county to Wheatley, five miles east of Oxford, when Hubert became vicar there.

Later, as shadow education secretary, Theresa May was one of six finalists in a pre-school learning competition when she wrote about her first day at Heythrop Primary School.

"I remember arriving at school screaming my head off because I didn't want to leave my mother," she wrote. "So I had to be carried into the class in the arms of the headmistress who announced to the rest of the class: 'Look what a silly little girl we've got here.'"

Heythrop Primary was a very small school with only twenty-seven pupils when she first went there. There were only eleven by the time she left.

"Mrs Williams, the headmistress, was the only teacher," May said. "I also remember that when the sun shone we used to take our desks outside, and sometimes when the ice cream van came we all got an ice cream if we had been very good."

Afterwards she spent a short time at St. Juliana's Convent School for Girls, a Roman Catholic independent school for would-be nuns in Begbroke, again just five miles from Oxford. The school has since closed. Tall for her age, she walked with her shoulders stooped because she was self-conscious about her height. She also admitted to being a swot at school.

"I shouldn't say it, but I probably was Goody Two Shoes," she confessed.

Her teenage pin-up was Geoffrey Boycott, having been brought up listening the Test matches with her father on the wireless.

"I have been a Geoff Boycott fan all my life," she said. "It was just that he kind of solidly got on with what he was doing."

She remained a lifelong fan and has attended cricket matches with her idol. In 2015, she supported a campaign to get Boycott knighted. "Sir Geoffrey" was denied an official knighthood because of his alleged assault of a former lover in 1996. Boycott denied the allegations, but still faced a £5,300 fine and three-month suspended sentence in France. Nevertheless, he remains her only admitted role model, though her father had certainly been influential.

"You don't think about it at the time, but there are certain responsibilities that come with being the vicar's daughter," she told the *Daily Telegraph*. "You're supposed to behave in a particular way."

Growing up in a rural vicarage, she would see her father working with the local community, speaking to his parishioners, listening to them and offering help when it was needed. One of her earliest memories was being with her mother in the kitchen when a family came up the garden path, demanding to see the vicar. The family would discuss current affairs at the dinner table. It was, she later remarked, "a natural environment to seek a political future". Altruism also was encouraged.

"You didn't think about yourself," she said. "The emphasis was on others."

She threw herself into village life, taking part in a pantomime that was produced by her father. With no siblings, she learnt self-reliance, tinged with a certain shyness, and she worked in the bakery on Saturdays to earn pocket money. Her strong Christian faith came from her upbringing and she went on to see politics as "a calling, a vocation... she doesn't think of it as work," said a friend.

While her father inspired in her a sense of public duty, "he was hopeless at cooking or mending a plug but hugely respected for his pastoral work," she said. "He visited one family and heard scrabbling noises in the house before the door was opened. When he sat down he put his hand over the armchair straight into a bowl of jelly and ice cream. They had been sitting eating and tried to clear it away before the vicar came in."

From the age of twelve, Theresa knew she wanted to be a politician and became a Conservative Party activist, but her father banned her canvassing for the Tories in the village to avoid accusations of political bias. Instead she stuffed envelopes in the local Conservative Party offices out of sight.

At thirteen, she moved on to Holton Park Girls' Grammar School in Wheatley. Two years later, this became Wheatley Park Comprehensive. Like St. Juliena's, the school was housed in an old manor house and was not without political significance. Holton House had been Oliver Cromwell's headquarters during the Civil War and was surrounded by extensive grounds. The girls' grammar had been set up there in 1948 and it had an excellent record of getting pupils into university at a time when few young women went on into further education.

Rosalind Hicks-Greene was at school with "Terri" and beat her in a mock election in 1974.

"It was not hard to beat Theresa as she was not very charismatic," Rosalind said. Nor has May changed much, according to Hicks-Greene. "The person you see on TV now is just a grown-up version of her seventeen-year-old self." She still has the same penchant for yellow, wearing a black suit with a flash of canary for her inaugural audience with the Queen.

The young Terri Braiser also lacked spontaneity. When history teacher started a debating society, pupils were asked to pick a topic for a two-minute talk of a hat. Theresa's subject was the school uniform. With no time to prepare, she found she had nothing to say. However, with schoolwork she was so capable and studious she was moved up a year. Her one act of rebellion at school was to challenge the head's ban on girls going a boys-only school trip to an international rugby match. In this, she had a father's backing.

Theresa went up to Oxford in to study geography at St. Hugh's College in October 1974. Contemporaries there remembered a tall, fashion-conscious young woman. Harold Wilson had just won the second general election of that year, giving Labour a slim majority and the Labour manifesto had promised a referendum on the UK membership of European Community, the forerunner of the EU. A bill would have to be passed as no such plebiscite had ever been held in Britain before, so politics were the talk of the university. But Theresa Brasier showed more interest than most.

"My memory's hazy but it was the first term at Oxford in 1974," recalled fellow first-year student Alicia Collinson. "We were at breakfast and she said something about wanting to be Prime Minister."

She was part of a high-flying set that also included Alan Duncan, who went on to become international development minister in Cameron's administration, and Damian Green, who answered to Mrs May at Home Office where he was minister of state for immigration, then minister of state for policing and criminal justice. He married Alicia Collinson, who went on to become a successful family law barrister.

Damian Green was considered the brightest of the set, and was thought to be destined for the highest office.

"I always wondered how it must have felt that Damian has been playing second fiddle to Theresa," said a friend.

6

Another contemporary was Michael Crick, the political correspondent for *Channel 4 News*.

So far no tales of drunken student revelry have come to light, but Collinson described the young Theresa as "fun" to spend time with, but others said that, even then, she was as "reticent and self-contained".

One contemporary told the *Daily Telegraph*: "You didn't feel you were ever on matey terms with Theresa, but Philip was easy to get on with."

Nevertheless, her university friend Pat Frankland and other friends insist that Theresa was not the dour figure she has later become, but had a full social life and a sense of fun, though still went to church every Sunday.

"It was quite high church stuff – there was nothing evangelical about Theresa, ever," said a friend. "It was good, solid religion."

That continued to this day.

"I am a vicar's daughter and still a practising member of the Church of England," she said forty years later. "It's right that we don't flaunt these things in British politics, but it is a part of me, it's there and it obviously helps to frame my thinking and my approach."

Even whilst wielding the axe on her first Sunday in Number Ten Downing Street, she found time to attend church in her constituency with her husband. Her Christian faith she explained, "is part of who I am and therefore how I approach things."

At university, she worked hard. In tutorials, a friend recalled she was "very determined and diligent – you know, she did what it said on the tin. She would do the work while I got drunk."

And she already had her eyes on the prize.

"I cannot remember a time when she did not have political ambitions," Frankland told the BBC. "I well remember, at the time, that she did want to become the first woman Prime Minister and she was quite irritated when Margaret Thatcher got there first."

Others recalled her expressing admiration for Mrs Thatcher, when she became leader of the opposition.

"I think the admiration was for what Thatcher was doing as a woman rather than her politics," a friend said. "I knew Theresa was interested in politics but there were no intimations back then that she would end up where she has."

However, they did not think she would go on to become Home Secretary, let alone Prime Minister.

It was said that, during the first two years of undergraduate life, Theresa had "many male friends but nobody who was special". St Hugh's was still a women-only college at the time while the rest of the university remained overwhelmingly male.

"We weren't girly," said a contemporary. "If you got into Oxford as a woman back then, you had a certain inner strength."

Chapter Two – The Darling Buds of May

Despite her studies, as a student Theresa did have time for boyfriends. According to Alicia Collinson: "Theresa went out with other people, but none of them were quite what she wanted. None of them were special. Then in our final year, Philip came along. There was Philip and nobody else."

Philip May was one year her junior, but had only just come up to Lincoln College when the couple were introduced at a Conservative Association disco by Benazir Bhutto, the future Prime Minister of Pakistani who was assassinated in 2007.

"It was at an Oxford University Conservative Association disco, of all the things, and I remember I was sitting talking to Benazir and Philip came over and she said 'oh, do you know Philip May?' and the rest is history, as they say," Theresa May told BBC Radio 4's *Desert Island Discs* programme in 2014. "He was good looking and there was an immediate attraction. We danced, though I can't remember the music."

Philip John May was born in Norfolk, but brought up on Merseyside where he attended Calday Grange Grammar School.

"He's a year younger than me and was two years… I was going to say behind me. He came up two years after me," said Theresa.

His mother Joy was a part-time French teacher at a girls' school, while his father was a sales rep for a shoe wholesaler – which later caused much amusement due to Theresa's penchant for exotic footwear. The couple soon learnt the surprising news that their future daughter-in-law had the ambition to become the next Mrs Thatcher.

Theresa was immediately impressed by Philip, confiding to a close friend: "There's a straightforward decency about him – sensible and unflash, but still steely, never to be underestimated."

They hit it off straight away, sharing and interest in politics and a sense of humour.

"Phil was a lot of fun," a friend told the *Guardian*. "He had loads of levity – but she did too. It's a myth she wasn't jolly because she was. She was good fun. She would come up with witticisms and quips. She would make jokes – a lot of them were cricketing jokes, to be fair."

The two of them bonded over their shared love of cricket. Theresa was known to have a soft spot for the West Indian fast bowler Tony Gray. She was also a fan of the comic trio Tim Brooke-Taylor, Graeme Garden and Bill Oddie.

"Theresa and I used to love watching *The Goodies*," said a university friend. "That was our sense of humour."

The series ran from 1970 to 1982. Since then she has become much more serious.

"She doesn't have a natural streak of piss-taking," said Sam Olsen, her campaign manager for the 2005 general election. "She's too serious-minded for that. If you tell a funny story, she'll laugh, but she doesn't tell stories herself."

On a work trip to the US, her special advisor Fiona Cunningham tried to get her to say the popular street-talk phrase "Oh no you didn't" in an American accent, accompanied by the necessary finger-pointing and head-twitching. Apparently May was game enough to try, but never quite loosened up enough to be convincing.

"She's very proper," said a colleague. "I suppose she's quite guarded."

Philip went on to become president of the Oxford Union, a post later held by Boris Johnson. Through the Union, he met the likes of disgraced US president Richard Nixon. However, according to Alan Duncan, Philip kept away from politics "for no other reason than that he had a different approach to life. Theresa was prepared to step into the light of public gaze. Philip preferred to be more in the background. It's as simple as that."

Despite her lacklustre performance at school, Theresa went on to become a keen debater. Reports of the Oxford Union debates at the time say she cut quite a figure. In one debate on abortion she is described as "the statuesque Miss Brasier burning with emotion in her red dress".

Along with her frequent appearances at the Union, she was also an active member of the Edmund Burke Society, an irreverent group that saw itself as the pretension-pricking antidote to the seriousness of university debating. The society held its debates on Sunday nights in the Morris Room at the Union, accompanied by copious amounts of port, swigged from tiny glasses.

In the third term of her final year at Oxford, she became president of the Edmund Burke Society and put down a series of light-hearted motions for debate. These included "That this House thanks Heaven for little girls", "That this House would" and "That Life's too short for chess". With due aplomb, she presided over proceedings using a meat tenderiser as a gavel. But this was the height of her ambition at university.

"She was very, very well-liked," said a friend. "I think part of the reason she never stood for election at the Union was that she wasn't a machinating politician. She wasn't somebody who would curry the support of different sides… She wasn't factional."

In 1977, she graduated with a second-class honours degree and took a job at the Bank of England, where she worked as an executive officer until 1983, while Philip stayed on at university. But she returned regularly to see Philip and sometimes found herself roped in to speak – notably opposing the motion "That sex is good… but success is better" in a debate organised by Philip in June 1978. Unfortunately, there is no record of her impassioned advocacy of the carnal act or whether her urgings persuaded the house. Theresa May has no notes in a dusty file.

"I always speak without notes," she said.

Asked during the 2016 leadership contest which side of the debate she would now be on, she said: "I'll plead the fifth amendment on that."

Things came to a head in 1979, Philip's final year. It seems that Theresa issued an ultimatum. After another student belle ditch her beau, the gossip column in the student newspaper *Cherwell* said: "I gather the same fate awaits Philip if he hesitates any longer in announcing his intention to make an honest woman of the Vicar's daughter."

That summer they got engaged. The following year, they were married in the Church of St Mary the Virgin in Wheatley, where her father was vicar.

The year after that, tragedy struck. The Reverend Hubert Brasier was driving his Morris Marina to a nearby church where he was due to conduct the evening Sunday service when he was in road traffic accident on the busy A40 outside Oxford. Crossing the central reservation, he edged forward into the path of a Range Rover. The driver tried to brake, but collided at high speed with the front wing. Sixty-four-year-old Braiser suffered head and spinal injuries. He was rushed to hospital, but could not be saved. He died a few hours later.

Theresa's mother, who suffered from multiple sclerosis and was confined to a wheelchair, went into rapid decline. A few months later she also died. At the age of twenty-five, Mrs May was suddenly lost both her parents.

While does not like to open up about personal matters, on *Desert Island Discs*, Theresa May told presenter Kirsty Young: "Crucially I had huge support in my husband and that was very important for me. I mean, he was a real rock for me, he has been all the time we've been married, but particularly then of course being faced with the loss of both parents within a relatively short space of time."

Alicia Collinson, who heard about the crash much later, said: "It was dreadful... Theresa had Philip and Philip saw her through that. He was and remains her rock."

The marriage endured, if anything strengthened. A colleague of Philip's in the City said that he was "absolutely devoted to Theresa and a little in awe of her". He was also happy to take on the Denis Thatcher role, being a hugely supportive, high-earning man prepared to carry the wife's handbag – indeed, in Philip May's case, actually choosing the handbag.

"Philip is very good at picking accessories," said Theresa.

With an MA in modern history, he became fund manager at stockbroker de Zoete & Bevan from 1979 to 1983 and Prudential Portfolio Managers UK from 1983 to 2000 and Deutsche Asset Management UK from 2000 to 2005. On LinkedIn, he lists his specialties as "UK Pension Fund relationship management" and "UK Insurance company relationship management". He has been a relationship manager at Capital Group, an American financial services company based in Belgravia, since December 2005. A spokesman said his job is to be a link with "personal clients in the UK, ensuring that they are happy with the service. He is not involved with, and doesn't manage, money and is not a portfolio manager. His job is to ensure the clients are happy with the service and that we understand their goals."

An associate described him as "an excellent colleague with strong strategic insights and a creative, thoughtful approach to investment. He is very much a team player."

He shares his wife's political view and was once chairman of the Wimbledon Conservative Association.

Another colleague said: "He often chairs meetings and does a very good job of making sure that everybody has their say. Around the office, he is a fairly head down type of guy. There is a stereotypical investment manager with a big ego – he's not like that at all. He is fairly quiet, keeps himself to himself. He has very good integrity and never trades off his wife's name."

After work, rather than drinking with other City types, he would head home.

"Philip is really lovely," said a friend. "He's just a regular, nice guy who's bright like she is. They still totally love each other and have a great friendship. He is good for her because he's aware she's Home Secretary but she's still just Theresa to him. They are not one of those couples where one of them is a big name and the other one quite likes it [the reflected glory]. That would never even come into his mind... When they're together, they seem younger."

When Theresa May became leader of the Conservative Party, the *Daily Mail* revelled in the idea that Philip May was going to be the new Denis Thatcher, though "without the G&Ts". Philip was said to be "not much of a drinker", though he enjoyed a glass of wine.

Noting his "well-developed, if rather wry, sense of humour", the *Mail* said: "It cannot be long before the satirical magazine *Private Eye* runs a column with echoes of 'Dear Bill', the imaginary letters from Mrs Thatcher's husband, Denis, to a golfing pal."

The "Bill" in question was supposed to have been Bill Deedes, former editor of the *Daily Telegraph*.

In the constituency he was her eyes and ears. He "listens to what people are saying and reports it all back to his wife". Philip Love, president of the local conservative association who had known the couple since May first arrived in the constituency, described Philip as "a really nice bloke who is very conscientious about his wife's work – the perfect partner to a Prime Minister."

Another friend in Berkshire said: "Philip would do anything for Theresa, but he's also her fiercest critic. He listens to her speeches very closely, so he can give her advice. He's good at dinner parties, easy to talk to – knowledgeable but not intense."

The fact that he was naturally reserved does no harm. A Conservative party source said: "Theresa May is the most unclubbable of politicians – and he is incredibly quiet. At party conferences, he is always three or four paces behind her and very happy not to be in the limelight."

The couple found they were unable to have children.

"It just didn't happen, so you know, it's, one of those things," she said.

They sought professional advice, to no avail – "I'd rather not go into details."

"Of course, we were both affected by it," she told *The Mail on Sunday*. "You see friends who now have grown-up children, but you accept the hand that life deals you. Sometimes things you wish had happened don't or there are things you wish you'd been able to do, but can't. There are other couples in a similar position."

It made them sad, but they drew comfort from their otherwise happy marriage.

Asked whether it had affected her outlook as a politician, she said: "I don't think so, it's an impossible question because you can't tell what you'd have been like if you'd been in a different position."

But she was stoical.

"I'm a great believer that you just get on with things. There are lots of problems people have. We are all different, we all have different circumstances and you have to cope with whatever it is, try not to dwell on things."

Chapter Three – A Definite Maybe

While Philip made his way in the world of finance, Theresa also continued working in the City. She was a financial consultant for the Inter-Bank Research Organisation from 1983 to 1985. Then she became head of the European Affairs Unit at the Association for Payment Clearing Services, until 1996, and Senior Adviser on International Affairs from 1996 to 1997. But she had already decided that her future lay in politics and, in 1985, she was elected as a local councillor in Merton, south London.

She served her ward for a decade, rising to become deputy leader of the council. As chairwoman of the local education committee, she ensured that teachers were paid at inner-London rates to protect the quality of the schools in the poorer part of the borough.

"She was very sound and very thorough," said council leader Harry Cowd.

That was also the verdict of Chris Grayling, who first met her when then were activists in southwest London.

"She and I are standing on the doorstep side by side, canvassing in a by-election in Wimbledon," he recalled. "At the end of it she told me off because I had only asked for the voting intention of the person who opened the door, not the rest of the household. That's Theresa. She's very thorough."

He went on to become her campaign manager in the leadership election and was rewarded with the post of transport secretary.

May was soon setting her sights even higher and began searching for a parliamentary constituency, failing at her first attempts to get selected as the Conservative candidate. But she was undaunted, later telling prospective politicians "there is always a seat out there with your name on it".

In 1992 election, she stood in the safe Labour seat of North West Durham, coming a distant second to Hilary Armstrong, who went on to become Labour's chief whip in Tony Blair's government. Her fellow candidates included the youthful Tim Farron, who went on to become leader of the Liberal Democrats. Armstrong polled 26,734, increasing her vote by 6.9 per cent. May took 12,767 votes, while Farron got 6,728, a dip of 6.1 per cent for the Lib Dems.

Two years later, May stood in Barking, east London, in a by-election. With the Conservative government at the depths of its unpopularity, she came third with just 1,976 votes, a slump of 23.5 per cent. Margaret Hodge took the seat with 13,704, a gain for Labour of 20.5 per cent. The Lib Dems' Gary White came second with 2,290.

The Conservatives' electoral fortunes hit their nadir in 1997. They were driven from power when Tony Blair came to power with a Labour landslide. However, Theresa May had been selected to stand for the new constituency of Maidenhead in Berkshire made up from parts of the seats of Windsor and Maidenhead, and Wokingham – both solid Tory heartlands.

Archive footage showed May out on the stump on a wet day in a raincoat and trilby. Asked what she though life in Westminster would entail, she said: "I haven't built up too many expectations. I think it's better to actually get there and find out. I have to get there yet."

But May was not a completely jejune.

"I obviously know the house a bit, because I have been in and out of it, prior to fighting this campaign," she said. "I think it is going to be a very interesting parliament next time around because there are going to be so many new faces... There have been a lot of MPs retiring on both sides of the house."

She also said that, during the election campaign, she had put everything else on hold.

"During the election campaign it is all out on the campaign trail, so everything else just doesn't happen a sense," she explained. "We have a phrase in our household which is ATE – after the election. Everything can happen after the election."

Though confident, she did not put any money on the result.

"I never bet on election victories," she said. "I'm sorry, I never bet on any election result."

She donned Tory blue on election night to hear the results being declared with her husband by her side. She won with 25,344 votes – some 49.8 of the poll and nearly twice that of the runner up, the Lib Dems' Andrew Ketteringham with 13,363. Labour's Denise Robson polled just 9,205.

May has held the seat ever since and improved on her 1997 majority of 11,981 in 2010 and 2015. Her majority now stands at 29,059, a massive 65.8 per cent of the vote.

"I wasn't expecting any particular margin," she said. "I don't like to predict election results, so I was just going for as many votes as we could."

Having won the election, she said she would put aside the Tory blue that had been her uniform through the campaign. In the house, she would dress the same as she did for business – in a smart suit.

"I like to wear a variety of colours," she said.

She did not think the party would pack her off to charm school and image-making classes to bush up her media appearance the way Mrs Thatcher had been. This was part of May's Conservative philosophy.

"In the Conservative Party we let people be more individualistic than the Labour Party does," she said. "They are the ones who send everyone to have their image made all the same. We actually let people be themselves."

The Mays were then living in nearby Sonning-on-Thames where their neighbours included Led Zeppelin guitarist Jimmy Page, ex-footballer Glenn Hoddle, and George and Amal Clooney. May said she was keen to continue being a regular commuter from Twyford. However, she realised that she was in for very long days, starting work at 8.30 in the morning handling the post, then after meetings, sometimes staying on until 10 or 10.30 at night for votes. So sometimes she would have to take the car.

When she turned up at the houses of parliament on her first day, she told ITV: "It is very exciting to be here, to be walking through these august corridors. But there is also here a sense of the tremendous responsibility you have as a member of parliament. I feel very much the history of the place."

However, as a new backbencher with the opposition, she found herself at the bottom of the pile when it came to the allocation of offices. On the Conservative Party website, she listed her proudest political achievement as a constituency MP bringing a minor injuries unit to St Mark's Hospital in Maidenhead and her interests as walking and cooking, and in the wildness years for the Conservative Party that followed, May was an early advocate of "modernisation".

Just a year after she was elected, party leader William Hague made her Shadow Spokesman for Schools, Disabled People and Women. Although not a flamboyant figure, she soon made her mark in that job. At the 1999 Conservative Party conference she promised "a bonfire of controls" to free schools from "the dead hand of local authorities". Later that year, she became the first of the 1997 intake to join the Shadow Cabinet as Shadow Secretary of State for Education and Employment.

Chapter Four – May Flowers

Following the 2001 election defeat, Theresa stayed in the Shadow Cabinet under the new leader Iain Duncan Smith and became Shadow Secretary of State for Transport, Local Government and the Regions. The following July, IDS appointed her the first female chairman of the Conservative Party with a brief to speed up party reform. It was in that role she quickly came to nationwide attention. Or at least her shoes did.

At her first Conservative Party Annual Conference as chairman her £110 Russell and Bromley leopard-print kitten heels dominated newspaper coverage. On the day after her opening speech, one third of the front page of the *Daily* Telegraph's front page was filled by a picture of her shoes and the accompanying headline read: "A stiletto in the Tories' Heart."

The newspaper noted that, while the chairman's address was usually a rallying call to the party faithful, laced with jibes about their opponents, May had broken with precedent and delivered a hard-hitting lecture on the unfavourable way the Tories were viewed by voters. The party was in disarray at the time. In the run-up to the Bournemouth conference, the headlines had been dominated by John Major's affair with Edwina Currie, Jeffery Archer's prison diaries and a whispering campaign against Duncan Smith's leadership.

Disgraced MP Jonathan Aitkin and Neil and Christine Hamilton were still doing the rounds.

Dressed in a black trouser suit, May acknowledged that the party had been damaged by recent scandals. Without naming names, she said: "A number of politicians have behaved disgracefully and then compounded their offences by trying to evade responsibility. We know who they are. Let's face it, some of them have stood on this platform."

Her criticism of her colleagues was withering.

"Some Tories have tried to make political capital by demonising minorities instead of showing confidence in all the citizens of our country," she said. "Some Tories have indulged themselves in petty feuding or personal sniping instead of getting behind a leader who is doing an enormous amount to change a party which has suffered two massive landslide defeats. Twice we went to the country unchanged, unrepentant, just plain unattractive. And twice we got slaughtered."

Her diagnosis was unrelenting.

"There's a lot we need to do in this party of ours," she said. "Our base is too narrow and so, occasionally, are our sympathies."

Then she delivered the coup de grâce.

"You know what some people call us?" she asked. "The nasty party."

There was no attempt to sugar the pill.

"I know that's unfair," she continued, "but it's the people out there we need to convince – and we can only do that by avoiding behaviour and attitudes that play into the hands of our opponents. No more glib moralising, no more hypocritical finger-wagging."

Local Conservative associates, she said, had to move with the time and select more ethnic minority and women candidates, rather than the usual fare of white, public school-educated men. She even heaped praise on Prime Minister Tony Blair for his efforts to disarm Saddam Hussein, rejecting Iain Duncan Smith's line that they should be more critical over the use of military action. And IDS had to sit through this. War was imminent. The previous week President George W. Bush had introduced the Joint Resolution to Authorize the Use of United States Armed Forces Against Iraq to the US Congress.

Commentators saw in her shoes a symbol of the way May wanted the party to change. Writing in the *Telegraph* Rachel Sylvester said: "There have been two Conservative parties on display in Bournemouth this week. The first wears leopard-print kitten heels, describes itself as conservatives.com and opens its arms to the voters in a welcoming embrace. The second prefers metaphorical bovver boots, defines itself as Britain plc and scowls that it is proud to be seen as the 'nasty party'."

Melissa Kite in *The Times* said: "The ditching of frumpy loafers in favour of sexy kitten heels may well turn out to be the Tories' Clause Four."

Within hours the shoe shop across the road from the conference centre had sold out of the "hot to trot" leopard-print shoes, along with most of the matching £199 leopard-print handbags called "foxy-trot". Hundreds had been sold. Russell & Bromley said that their switchboard was jammed and they were swamped with demand from Tory strongholds such as Winchester and Guildford.

"By Tory standards the shoes are racy," wrote Kite. "As well as having spiky heels and silky leopard print, their leather soles are engraved with the words: 'In love the chase is better than the catch. Too much is not enough'."

The political ramifications of the shoes were plain for all to see.

"When the history of the Conservative Party is written it may record that the Tory revival began not in Bournemouth International Conference Centre but in a shoe shop across the road," said *The Times*.

The next day, she wore "multi-coloured velvet pair of Mary-Janes". Later in the week, there were "a pair of "pinstriped black shoes with the red rose of Labour on the instep". These were compared to Kenneth Clarke's perennial brown suede shoes and Duncan Smith's "expensive-looking but well-worn pair of classic black brogues, polished to a military sheen".

Meanwhile the left-leaning *Daily Mirror* commented that she was playing on Conservative MPs "dominatrix fantasy, with her formidable, finger-wagging, headmistress act".

"The sight of Theresa May in kitten-heeled leopard skin 'don't f*** with me' shoes was enough, apparently, to bring tears to the eyes of red- blooded Tories on the first day of the party conference," it said. And the offenders would be "queuing up outside her study for a closer inspection of those goolie-kickers".

Others said that male MPs were in "a collective lather" experiencing a "quiver of excitement", not unlike their reaction to Margaret Thatcher. Andrew Marr pointed out that some of them were "not wholly averse to a little public humiliation from a good-looking woman".

Her leather jacket also drew attention. The *Sun* said that she was giving the party's image a re-vamp – "Presumably she thinks leopard-skin heels and a leather jacket will attract a new type of Tory." More cruelly, the *Guardian* said that the red leather jacket gave her an "ageing, faintly upmarket hooker pose".

May responded: "It beats me why the *Guardian* knows what an upmarket hooker looks like."

Somehow Christine Keeler got dragged into the debate. The *Guardian* then issued a clarification.

"We were not suggesting any resemblance to someone as sexy and high-maintenance as Ms Keeler," said the newspaper, "more with the sort of game-yet-battle-scarred old bird of the sort once popular with one of Mrs May's central office predecessors, who hangs round Shepherd Market in the hope of a bottle of chablis and a quick tumble in a three-star hotel."

But the newspapers would not let the shoes drop.

"It is quite widely known that I like shoes," she said. "This is not something that defines me as either a woman or a politician, but it has come to define me in the eyes of the newspapers. I wore a pair of leopard-print kitten heels to a Conservative Party Conference a few years ago and the papers have continued to focus on my feet ever since."

The dominatrix image also followed her around. The following year *The Times* said that May was "known as Miss Whiplash by fellow party members for her black leather skirts and sexy, red kitten heels". In an interview that may appear to some to be shocking sexist, she was asked what was in her make-up bag.

The answer was a lot of Helena Rubenstein. She used Rubenstein's foundation and lipstick – namely Spirituality – and used Rubenstein Vitamin C cream as a moisturiser. And she always put make-up on before going out, except if she was going to the gym.

May described herself as a low-maintenance woman. She had her hair cut in a salon in her constituency and had no time for manicures and facials, though she did exercise regularly. She did not believe in Brazilians and would, if she could, have white socks banned by the fashion police.

Asked for the three words that defined her style, she said confident, elegant and practical. Her most recent purchase was a pink silk jacket, bought on a long weekend in Paris. At work she work skirts and trouser suits – "although I am known for a black leather skirt and a red leather jacket (not worn together)". She also said she liked the cut of the clothes designed by Amanda Wakeley.

Sixty was the age limit for wearing a micro-mini shirt – "though, I'd say if you have the legs, go for". May was just forty-seven then, but had yet to shock the party faithful by flashing her thighs. Given the reaction to her attire at the party conference, it was probably as well. Best not risk backbenchers getting overexcited.

Of course, questions about shoes could not be avoided long and May brought up the subject by admitting that her greatest sartorial embarrassment was a pair of lime-green platforms she had worn as a teenager. Her greatest extravagance, she confessed, were shoes Beverly Feldman at Russell & Bromley and L.K. Bennett.

"At 5ft 11in, I favour kitten heels because they're practical and comfortable but still flatter the leg," she explained.

She bought them in shoe shops in her constituency and picked up tips from *Vogue* and *Harpers & Queen*, though she was not in favour of judging the book by the covers.

"In politics image is very important," she said, "but you should take time to look between the covers."

And British men could not get casual clothes right – "too many bad jumpers."

She said she holidayed in Italy and walking in Switzerland, and thought that Isabella Rossellini the most beautiful woman in the world. If there was one part of her body that she would change, it would be her hands and her greatest regret was not learning the piano when her mother tried to teach her. Her motto was "don't let the bastards grind you down". Which was fortunate as it is hard to imagine a male politician being interviewed in such a fashion. It was a mark of the woman that she did not take offence and was happy to be seen as a womanly woman, confident that she was being taken seriously as a politician elsewhere. After all, while her exuberant choice of footwear had become her trademark, she has a more enduring claim to fame from the 2002 conference where she first stepped into the limelight. The *Oxford Book of Modern Quotations* now includes the snippet from her speech saying: "You know what some people call us: the nasty party."

In July 2003, her political statue was recognised when she became a member of the Privy Council.

When Michael Howard took over the leadership of the Conservative Party in November 2003, he nearly halved the size of the Shadow Cabinet, slimming it down to just twelve. Theresa May remained in it, becoming shadow secretary of state for transport and the environment. In June 2004, she was moved to become Shadow Secretary of State for Culture, Media and sport.

In the 2001, her majority had shrunk to 3,284, so the Lib Dems targeted her as one of the five top Tory in their so-called decapitation strategy in the 2005 general election. The others were shadow chancellor Oliver Letwin, Shadow Education Secretary Tim Collins, Shadow Home Secretary David Davis and Michael Howard himself whose 5,907 majority, Lib Dem leader Charles Kennedy said, was not secure. The plan was to throw resources in to unseat these big beasts. The Lib Dems were banking on a late switch of Labour voters, possibly motivated by the war in Iraq, to topple at least some big Tory figures. While Labour's majority in the House of Commons was cut from 167 to 66, the Lib Dems only gained an extra eleven seats. Of the five targeted, only Tim Collins lost his seat – to future Lib Dem leader Tim Farron. Theresa May increased her majority to

6,231, while the Lib Dem candidate in her constituency, Kathryn Newbound, put on just 859 at the expense of Labour and the Monster Raving Loony Party.

However, the Conservatives had lost the 2005 election and Michael Howard was replaced by David Cameron who appointed May Shadow Leader of the House of Commons, even though she was conspicuously not part of the "Notting Hill set" that brought Cameron and George Osborne to power.

In his conference speech that year, Cameron said that, among other things, the Conservative Party had "lost support amongst women". This inspired May and Baroness Jenkin of Kennington to start Women2Win that helped train and support female candidates. In 2005, there were just seventeen women Conservative MPs. That went up to forty-nine in 2010 and sixty-eight in 2015, with women beating Vince Cable, Mark Reckless and Ed Balls. May had always opposed all-women shortlists, insisting that all her political achievements were the result of her own efforts and abilities, regardless of gender.

"As a Tory woman, I'm instinctively suspicious of positive discrimination," she said. "I'm a passionate believer in meritocracy."

On her advent to office, a former colleague said: "She's not going to be part of any boys' club because a) she's not a boy and b) she wouldn't want to be a member of any club anyway... I don't think she would ever want to be seen to make her sex an excuse for anything. She didn't treat me as a woman, she treated me as a person. Her beef with Harriet Harman [the Labour deputy leader] is

'Don't play victim'. You just do your job really well and then you can punch at the same weight a man can."

In January 2009, May was made Shadow Secretary of State for Work and Pensions. That May, the expenses scandal broke in the *Daily Telegraph*, resulting in four parliamentarians being jailed for false accounting. Mrs May, of course, was above reproach. Her website said: "Theresa has one of the lowest expenses claims of any MP and her main home has always been the Maidenhead constituency. She has never claimed for food, furniture or household goods and has always been a full-time MP. However, Theresa believes that all MPs should apologise for the system of expenses that developed and allowed abuse to take place."

Chapter Five – May Flies

In 2010, the Tories took power in coalition with the Lib Dems with Theresa May increasing her majority again, to 16,769. On 12 May 2010, she joined the cabinet as Home Secretary and Minister for Women and Equality. She was only the fourth woman to hold one of the Great Offices of State in Britain. The others were the previous Home Secretary Jacqui Smith, Margaret Beckett who was foreign secretary from May 2005 to June 2007, and Margaret Thatcher, who was Prime Minister from May 1979 to November 1990.

Her appointment was something of a surprise as Chris Grayling and been Shadow Home Secretary while the Conservatives were in opposition. He became Minister of State for Employment, later secretary of state for Justice and Lord Chancellor, Lord President of the Council, Leader of the House of Commons and, after being May's campaign manager for during the leadership race, though a Brexiteer, Secretary of State for Transport.

The Home Office has turned out to be the political graveyard of many a politician, but May went on to become the longest serving Home Secretary for over sixty years. Former Lib Dem MP David, who was Chief Secretary to the Treasury in the coalition said: "I first met her in 2010. I was sitting in my Treasury office, overlooking St James's Park, me in one armchair and the Home Secretary in the other, with no officials present. She looked nervous. I felt she was surprised to find herself as Home Secretary. Frankly, I didn't expect her to last more than a couple of years."

She clung on by mastering her brief with what was said to be a microscopic attention to detail. Meanwhile she was happy to join battle with other ministers when she thought it necessary.

David Laws recalled: "She would frequently clash with George Osborne over immigration. She rarely got on anything but badly with Michael Gove. She and Cameron seemed to view each other with mutual suspicion."

She also had a run-in with Vince Cable, business secretary in the coalition, over immigration.

"In cold and icy terms she took him apart," said Damian Green. "And I had the strong impression that nobody had ever spoken to Vince like that before. He almost physically shrank. This was a strong woman getting her way at least partly just by force of personality."

Some in Downing Street worried that the Home Office was becoming her own personal fiefdom because of the loyalty she engendered among her ministers and, despite her frosty relationship with Cameron, was regarded as "unmovable" as her tough-talking style met with public approval even when the department's record did not always seem so strong.

Indeed, she regularly clashed with Number Ten. According to a former Downing street aide: "The operational style – the way that her spads [special advisers] operated – it was a sort of a bunker-ish mentality, that involved lots of briefing against other departments and Number Ten."

When May took over has Home Secretary, her predecessor Jacqui Smith left her a letter saying: "Please try to resist those who say police numbers do not count – they do. Some senior police voices will try to suggest too much emphasis has been place on neighbourhood policing and building confidence. They are wrong."

One of her first assignments as Home Secretary was to go on the beat in the Winstanley estate in Clapham alongside Sir Paul Stephenson, commissioner of the Metropolitan Police. Sir Paul listed the challenges facing her, which included counter-terrorism, combating organised crime and ensuring security at the 2012 Olympic Games.

As Home Secretary, she was also a member of the National Security Council, a cabinet committee set up by Cameron to oversee intelligence, defence and national security. Her security brief brought her into conflict with Lib Dem leader and deputy Prime Minister Nick Clegg, particularly over her plan to increase internet surveillance to combat terrorism, which the Lib Dems dubbed the "Snooper's Charter".

After one difficult meeting with her Clegg reportedly told David Laws: "You know, I've grown to rather like Theresa May… She's a bit of an Ice Maiden and has no small talk whatsoever – none. I have quite difficult meetings with her. Cameron once said, 'She's exactly like that with me too!'"

Their judgement was that she was instinctively secretive and very rigid, but you could be tough with her and she would go away and think through her position again. They were forced to conceded that, under May, the country avoided any mass terrorist attack and crime levels in the UK fell, something she put down to the government slashing red tape and scrapping targets which enabled the police to focus on crime fighting, as well as setting up a College of Policing to ensure the police are better equipped with the knowledge and skills they need to fight crime.

She was known for her steely glare in confrontations with fellow ministers around the Cabinet table.

"I remember a couple of Cobra [the government's emergency Cabinet Office Briefing Room] meetings when Theresa did not hide her irritation with other ministers," said an insider. "There would be tutting and rolling of eyes, particularly to more junior ministers."

However, she was "incredibly well respected, but not liked. The opposite of Boris."

The workload at the Home Office was heavy and the post also came with a threat to her personal security from extremists. When she was first appointed to the job, a parliamentary colleague who had known May for more than a decade remembers asking her how it was going.

"She looked at me and said, 'The stuff that goes across your desk...' and I could see, etched across her face, how overwhelming the role was from the outside, the risk that has to be borne."

Her first bold move as Home Secretary was to halt the extradition of Gary McKinnon. He was accused of hacking into ninety-seven American military and NASA computers, causing damage the US government claims cost more than $700,000 dollars to repair. He admitted breaching the security of these sensitive systems but denied causing damage, claiming that he was looking for evidence of UFOs. A judicial review had found that forty-four-year-old McKinnon, who was autistic, was in danger of committing suicide if he was extradited. Mrs May said she would re-examine the medical evidence before making a decision.

May was seemingly unafraid of incurring the wrath of the US and McKinnon's mother Janis Sharp said: "She says what she thinks and is very brave."

On 16 October 2012, May announced to the House of Commons that the extradition had been permanently blocked, saying that "Mr McKinnon's extradition would give rise to such a high risk of him ending his life that a decision to extradite would be incompatible with Mr McKinnon's human rights". However, the Director of Public Prosecutions should determine whether McKinnon should face trial before a British court. On 14 December, the DPP Keir Stammer announced that McKinnon would not be prosecuted in the UK due to the difficulty of bringing a case against him when the evidence was in the United States. May was widely praised for sticking up to the might of the US.

Another bold initiative was the abolition of the National Identity Card scheme introduced by Tony Blair's government in 2006. She had been in office just two weeks when she introduced the Identity Documents Act which cancelled all existing ID cards, prevented the issuing of new ones and closed down the National Identity Register, destroying its records. Migrant workers from outside the EU and thousands of British citizens in the North-West of England, where the scheme was being piloted, have already been issued with cards.

She also proposed the reform of the DNA database, tighter regulation of CCTV and a review of libel laws due to what was seen as the erosion of civil liberties under the Labour government.

"We will be scrapping ID cards but also introducing an annual cap on the number of migrants coming into the UK from outside the European Union," she said. She also planned to introduce elected police commissioners and cut paperwork to give the police more time on the streets.

On the DNA database, she said: "We are absolutely clear we need to make some changes in relation to the DNA database. For example, one of the first things we will do is to ensure that all the people who have actually been convicted of a crime and are not present on it are actually on the DNA database. The last government did not do that. It focused on retaining the DNA data of people who were innocent. Let's actually make sure that those who have been found guilty are actually on that database."

On 2 June 2010, May faced her first major national security incident as Home Secretary with the Cumbria shootings when fifty-year-old taxi driver Derrick Bird shot and killed his brother, solicitor and a fellow cab-driver, and wounded two other cab-drivers and a passenger, before driving around the area randomly shooting at people, then killing himself. It was the worst mass shooting in the UK since Dunblane, when Thomas Hamilton killed sixteen children and their teacher in an attack on their school in Scotland in 1996.

Therese May paid tribute to those involved, saying: "I have spoken to Craig Mackey, the chief constable of Cumbria, on a few occasions today. He updated me on the very serious and tragic events in Cumbria. As the Prime Minister said earlier today, our thoughts are with the friends and families of the victims. I should like to pay tribute to the way that the police and emergency services have worked closely together in dealing with this terrible incident. This is clearly an ongoing investigation so it would not be appropriate for me to comment on the details. It is right that the facts should come from the police and they will release further details as appropriate. However, they have already confirmed that twelve people have been killed and at least twenty-five people have been injured."

The following day, she addressed the House of Commons.

"Undoubtedly, yesterday's killings will prompt a debate about our country's gun laws, that is understandable and indeed it is right and proper," she said. "But it would be wrong to react before we know the full facts. Today we must remember the innocent people who were taken from us as they went about their lives, then, we must allow the police time to complete their investigations."

She stressed that such mass killings were extreme rare in Britain.

"That doesn't make it any the less painful, and it doesn't mean we shouldn't do everything we can to stop it happening again," she said.

"Where there are lessons to be learned, we will learn them. Where there are changes to be made, we will make them."

May then accompanied the Prime Minister on a visit to Cumbria to meet the police officers involved in the incident and visit surviving victims in hospital.

She continued cutting back bureaucracy set up by Labour with the suspension of the registration scheme for the nine million carers working with children and vulnerable adults, due to begin in that July. The Vetting and Barring Scheme was seen to be "disproportionate and overly burdensome, and that it unduly infringes on civil liberties". May called it "draconian".

In a statement, she said: "The safety of children and vulnerable adults is of paramount importance to the new government. However, it is also vital that we take a measured approach in these matters. We've listened to the criticisms and will respond with a scheme that has been fundamentally remodelled. Vulnerable groups must be properly protected in a way that is proportionate and sensible. This redrawing of the vetting and barring scheme will ensure this happens."

She told the BBC: "You were assumed to be guilty until you were proven innocent, and told you were able to work with children. All sorts of groups out there were deeply concerned about this and how it was going to affect them. There were schools where they were very concerned that foreign exchanges could be finished as a result of this, parents were worried about looking after other people's children after school."

May then banned the Indian Muslim preacher Zakir Naik from entering the United Kingdom for what she called his "unacceptable behaviour". The radical preacher lived in Mumbai and worked for Peace TV. While a recognised authority on Islam, he was known for making disparaging remarks about other religions and was due to give a series of lectures in London and Sheffield.

"Numerous comments made by Dr Naik are evidence to me of his unacceptable behaviour," she said. "Coming to the UK is a privilege, not a right and I am not willing to allow those who might not be conducive to the public good to enter the UK. Exclusion powers are very serious and no decision is taken lightly or as a method of stopping open debate on issues."

Dr Naik was the first person she had excluded.

May also announced plans for a temporary cap on UK visas for non-EU migrants. She planned to limit the number or workers entering the county to 24,100 between the end of June and the following April, a fall of five per cent. Again she crossed swords with Deputy Prime Minister Nick Clegg, who denounced the move. It also rankled education secretary Michael Gove and David Willetts, the minister for universities and science, who privately warned her that too rigid a formula could undermine Britain's appeal to foreign business leaders and overseas students. Their anxieties are shared by influential voices in the City, industry and higher education.

Concluding a busy month, she told the conference of the Association of Chief Police Officers that cuts to the Home Office budget would result in a reduction in police numbers. Nevertheless, "frontline availability should increase even as budgets contract," she said.

She also announced she was scrapping immediately the performance targets and minimum standards introduced by Labour and would press on with her plan for locally-elected police commissioners.

Chapter Six – Mayhem

In July 2010, May presented the House of Commons with proposals for a fundamental review of the previous Labour government's security and counter-terrorism legislation, including "stop and search" powers. She also intended to review the twenty-eight-day limit on detaining terrorist suspects without charge as the existing powers had been misused or had encroached on civil liberties.

"This review will enable this government to put right the failures of the last government," she said. "In doing so, it will restore the ancient civil liberties that should be synonymous with the name of our country."

Again she appeared to be a champion of liberty.

On 26 July 2010, May announced in the House of Commons a package of reforms to policing in England and Wales. The police had "become too bureaucratic, too much accountable to Whitehall, rather than to the people they're serving," she said and proposed the "most radical reform of policing for fifty years".

The key changes included the scrapping of Police Authorities in England and Wales. Instead, elected police and crime commissioners would have the power to hire and fire chief constables from May 2012. She proposed the introduction of police reservists – a pool of volunteers to undertake police duties. There would also be "community crime fighters" – ordinary people could take part in joint patrols with officers. There will also be a campaign for more special constables and a membership drive for Neighbourhood Watch schemes. This was in line with the Conservative manifesto call for the "Big Society" and its renewed emphasis on voluntary action.

The National Policing Improvement Agency would be phases out and the Serious Organised Crime Agency (SOCA) would be abolished after it was shown that, every £15 of public money it spent, it recovered just £1 from criminals. Instead there would be a new UK-wide National Crime Agency, which would specialise in organised crime and border policing, and incorporate the child exploitation and online protection centre.

She also proposed a review to overturn the Labour government's anti-social behaviour legislation and abolish Anti-Social Behaviour Orders, or ASBOs, which were not working. More than half of them had been breached between 2000 and 2008, often many times over, and were seen as "badge of honour" among teenage offenders.

"We need a complete change in emphasis, with people and communities working together to stop bad behaviour escalating," she said. "We need to make anti-social behaviour what it once was – abnormal and something to stand up to… rather than frequent and tolerated. Anti-social behaviour still blights lives, wrecks communities and provides a pathway to criminality. It might sometimes feel like an unwinnable battle but it's not. There is nothing inevitable about crime and there is nothing inevitable about anti-social behaviour. By coming together, and only by coming together, we can win this battle."

In August, she scraped the Labour government's proposed "go orders", a scheme to protect women from domestic violence by banning abusers from the victim's home as part of the drive to cut public spending. Under the scheme, senior police would have been given the power to act instantly to safeguard families they considered at threat. Violent men would have been banned from their homes for up two weeks, giving their victims the chance to seek help to escape abuse. It was due to be piloted that autumn and rolled out the following year. May said she had taken the decision to scrap it to save money and because of worries about the legislation setting up the orders. The Home Office was under pressure to cut at least £2.5 billion from its annual budget of £10 billion.

She followed this by scrapping ContactPoint, the £224-million government database of all eleven million children in the UK set up by the Labour administration in the wake of the Victoria Climbié, the eight-year-old who had died in 2000 after months of abuse. Launched in 2009 it held the names and addresses of all under-eighteen-year-olds, along with the contact details of their parents, schools and GPs. Police officers, social workers and teachers had access to, but the controversial system was beset with delays, technical problems and fears over security.

Government cutbacks caused social unrest which, as Home Secretary, May had to deal with. Students took to the streets to protest the increase in tuition fees. They vandalised the Supreme

Court, broke into the Treasury building in Whitehall and attacked a car carrying Prince Charles and Camilla. May came under pressure to deploy water cannon. That was a matter for the police, she maintained.

"Whether or not they choose to use water cannon is an operational issue," she told Sky News. "I think it is right that we look across the board at all the options that are available. It is a matter for them to decide which tactics they wish to use. They will look across the board at the powers that are available to them, at the operational things that they can do and make decisions to ensure any future demonstrations that take place are also policed robustly."

Policing again became an issue following the TUC anti-cuts march on 26 March 2011. While up to half-a-million people attended a rally in Hyde Park, a members of the group UK Uncut occupied Fortnum & Mason's store in Piccadilly, protesting against the alleged tax avoidance by the company's owners. Some 138 were arrested for aggravated trespass, though the charges were later dropped.

Other black-clad protesters sprayed graffiti on police vehicles and shops in Oxford street and smashed windows. Banks, Topshop, the Ritz Hotel and the Porsche dealership in Mayfair were among the targets. Eleven arrests were made and clashes between the protesters and police continued into the night in Trafalgar Square.

The following day in the House of Commons, May rallied to the police defence, saying that fifty-six officers had been injured – twelve of whom had required hospital treatment – along with fifty-three members of the public. Of the two hundred demonstrators arrested 149 had been charged.

"The message to those who carry out violence is clear," she said. "You will be caught and you will be punished."

She praised off for learning the lessons of the tuition-fees protests the previous year, where protestors occupied the Conservative Party headquarters and were kettle by riot police in Millbank Square, resulting in violent clashes.

"The police might not have managed to prevent every act of violence but they were successful in preventing wider criminality and are now actively engaged in investigating the perpetrators so that they can be brought to justice," she said. "Just as the police review their operational tactics, so we in the Home Office will review the powers available to the police. I am willing to consider powers which would ban known hooligans from rallies and marches and I will look into the powers the police already have to force the removal of face coverings and balaclavas. If the police need more help to do their work, I will not hesitate in granting it to them."

He also threatened to given the police new powers to crack down the social media protesters were using to organise their demonstrations.

In the summer of 2011, rioting broke out in several London boroughs and across the country following the death of Mark Duggan who had been shot dead in Tottenham on 4 August. The result was five deaths and over £200 million worth of property damage. Over three thousand people were arrested and the courts and to sit extended hours.

"I condemn utterly the violence in Tottenham," she said. "Such disregard for public safety and property will not be tolerated and the Metropolitan Police have my full support in restoring order."

May flew back from holiday to meet the police and executives from social media networks to see how they could help prevent them being used for criminal behaviour. But she did not did not seek any additional powers to close down networks such as BlackBerry Messenger, Facebook or Twitter when disorder broke out, though it was clear that some incidents had been prompted by the use of messaging services. Nor did she call for the use of water cannon on the British mainland. The police would have needed her consent to bring them over from Northern Ireland.

"The way we police in Britain is not through use of water cannon," she said. "The way we police in Britain is through consent of communities."

She also told BBC *Breakfast* that "parents need to be asking themselves where were their children, what were their children doing in the evening."

She added: "There are longer-term questions about when we see parents letting their children as young as that sort of age be out on the streets in this way."

Around one in five of those who have appeared in court are under eighteen and at one stage last week as many as half of those who had gone through London courts were juveniles a consequently were given anonymity by the courts – even though four of them posed in front of £3,000-worth of good they had looted for a national newspaper.

"When I was in Manchester last week, the issue was raised to me about the anonymity of juveniles who are found guilty of crimes of this sort," she said once order had been restored. "What I've asked is that CPS guidance should go to prosecutors to say that where possible, they should be asking for the anonymity of juveniles who are found guilty of criminal activity to be lifted."

Theresa May had always been tough on immigration. In 2010 she promised to bring the level of net migration down to less than 100,000 and at the Conservative Party Conference in October 2011, she argued that the Human Rights Act "needs to go". To illustrate the point, she said: "We all know the stories… about the illegal immigrant who cannot be deported because, and I am not making this up, he had a pet cat."

Within minutes, a spokesman for the Judicial Office at the Royal Courts of Justice, which issues statements on behalf of senior judges, said: "This was a case in which the Home Office conceded that they had mistakenly failed to apply their own policy – applying at that time to that appellant – for dealing with unmarried partners of people settled in the UK. That was the basis for the decision to uphold the original tribunal decision – the cat had nothing to do with the decision."

The cat had only come up at the original tribunal as part of the evidence showing that the defendant has a genuine relationship with his partner in the UK – they owned a cat together.

Justice Secretary Ken Clarke told the BBC: "The cat surprised me. I cannot believe anyone was refused deportation just because they owned a cat."

Later he told a fringe meeting that the case "certainly has nothing to do with the Human Rights Act and nothing to do with the European Convention on Human Rights". He also pointed out that repealing the UK Human Rights Act would mean "all the cases go back to Strasbourg", adding: "I think it is a good idea that we remain adhering to the Convention on Human Rights and the cases are heard here by British judges."

May defended her comments about the cat, telling the BBC her speech had been checked before it went out. Besides, this case was just one example of where she believed the law was being misconstrued. But she promised she would have another look at the detail. It was then discovered that the source of the cat story was Nigel Farage. Clarke concluded that May's comments were "laughable and childlike".

Nevertheless, May's conference speech was only a foretaste of the statement on family migration she made in the House of Commons on 11 June 2012.

"The government are committed to reviewing all the main routes for immigration to the UK as part of our programme to reform the immigration system," she said. "As a result, we anticipate that net migration will fall from the hundreds of thousands to the tens of thousands. We have already announced major changes to the immigration rules by introducing a cap on work visas and reforming student visas to cut out widespread abuse. We now turn to reform of the family route."

She then outlined the abuses she had identified.

"Sham marriages have been widespread, people have been allowed to settle in Britain without being able to speak English, and there have not been rules in place to stop migrants becoming a burden on the taxpayer. We are changing all that. The UK needs a system for family migration that is underpinned by three simple principles: first, that those who come here should do so on the basis of a genuine relationship; secondly, that migrants should be able to pay their way; and thirdly, that they are able to integrate into British society. If people do not meet those requirements, they should not be allowed to come here."

New rules would come into effect on 9 July.

"For too long we have had an immigration system that could be easily exploited by sham relationships," she continued. "We are stepping up our enforcement activity, but it is important that policy reflects the seriousness of the problem as well. We will therefore increase the minimum probationary period for new spouses and partners from two years to five years. We will also publish new guidance to help caseworkers identify sham marriages.

"For too long we have had an immigration system that did not take into account whether people coming here could pay their way. The government's reforms will mean that anyone who wishes to bring a foreign spouse or partner, or dependants to Britain will have to be able to support them financially. They must not become a burden on the taxpayer. Following advice from the Migration Advisory Committee, we will set a minimum income threshold of £18,600 for sponsoring a partner to settle in the UK. This is the level at which a sponsor can generally support themselves and a partner without accessing income-related benefits. Children involve additional costs for the state. To reflect this, there will be a higher threshold for each child sponsored: a £22,400 threshold for a partner with one child, with an additional £2,400 for each further child."

She would also crack down on elderly relatives joining their migrant children as a potential burden on the taxpayer.

"If someone wants to sponsor, a dependent relative to come to Britain who requires personal care, they will have to show, first, that they cannot organise care in the relative's home country and, secondly, that they can look after the relative without recourse to public funds. We will also limit to close family the people who are able to access that route: parents, grandparents, sons, daughters, brothers and sisters. Aunts and uncles will no longer be eligible to come here through the family route. Future applications will also have to be made from overseas, not while the applicant is here as a visitor."

She also wanted to stop the influx of people who did not understand English or the British way of life.

"From October 2013, all those who wish to live here will need to demonstrate that they are able to participate fully in British life. All applicants for settlement will need to pass the "Life in the UK" test and, because a person cannot integrate if they cannot communicate, we are strengthening the language requirement by introducing a separate English language test at intermediate level."

This was a direct challenge to Article 8 of the European Convention on Human Rights, which guarantees the right to respect for private and family life, but May insisted that this was a "qualified right" which the courts had been left to interpret without the guidance of parliament. Serious criminals would also be deported.

"If a foreign criminal has received a custodial sentence of twelve months or more, deportation will normally be proportionate. Even if a criminal has received a shorter sentence, deportation will still normally be proportionate if their offending has caused serious harm or if they are a persistent offender who shows particular disregard for the law. For the most serious foreign criminals – those sentenced to four or more years in prison – Article 8 rights will prevent deportation only in the most exceptional of circumstances."

She had laid down the law, not just in the House of Commons but also, as Yvette Cooper pointed out, in advance in *The Sunday Times* and on *The Andrew Marr Show*.

She was challenged by the All-Party Parliamentary Group on Migration who took submissions from nearly three hundred families and found that the new rules would force British citizens into indefinite exile and separate young children from their parents.

"We also heard that the new rules may have generated costs to the public purse, which we assume must not have been anticipated," their report said.

May's views on the Human Rights Act got her in trouble with the law in June 2012 when she became only the second Home Secretary to be found in contempt of court, having failed to honour an undertaking to release a fail asylum seeker.

"We also consider it likely that the Home Secretary's intemperate comments about the Human Rights Act and the perceived failings of the judiciary gave rise to a culture within UK Border Agency in which her officials failed to abide by the rule of law," the judge said. During his time in detention he had made several suicide attempts.

However, no penalty was imposed for the contempt as the finding itself was serious.

"We believe that the finding that the refusal to honour the undertaking was contempt of court was in part designed to ensure that there is no future repetition of this conduct on their part," the judge said. The asylum seeker had since been released, so May avoided any further sanctions, but the judge ruled that the detainee was entitled to damages.

The other occasion when a Home Secretary was found in contempt of court was in 1991 when Kenneth Baker ignored an instruction from a judge in an asylum case and the ruling against him was backed up by five law lords in a landmark judgment.

Chapter Seven – Definitely Maybe

As well as being Home Secretary, Theresa May was Minister for Women and Equality from May 2010 until September 2012, when the job was taken over by Maria Miller, who also became Culture Secretary in David Cameron's first major cabinet reshuffle. May's appointment had long been criticised by the Lesbian, Gay, Bisexual and Transgendered lobby. In 1998 she had voted against equalising the age of consent and, in 2000, she had also voted against the repeal of Clause 28 of the 1988 Local Government Act which banned the "promotion" of homosexuality by local government and schools. In 2001 and 2002 she voted against gay couples jointly adopting children.

In 2004, like much of the Conservative front bench, she did vote in favour of civil partnerships. That same year, though, she did not attend parliament for any of the four votes on the Gender Recognition Act that allowed transsexuals full legal recognition of their new gender. However, taking office in 2010, she had changed her mind on many of these matters.

"If those votes were today, yes, I have changed my view and I think I would take a different vote," she said.

Launching a document setting out the coalition government's position on LGBT rights, she told *PinkNews*: "Cultural change is not straightforward, but it is essential to advance the cause of LGB and

T rights. Of course there is a role for politicians here too and I'm proud that this election saw an increase in the number of openly gay MPs in parliament, although we have further to go."

Her proposals included allowing gay people to have religious civil partnerships and removing historical convictions for consensual gay sex from criminal records. She also said that she would press ahead with a streamlined version of the Labour government's anti-discrimination laws, despite having opposed them in opposition on the grounds to many of the bill's clauses were too bureaucratic and expensive. It would ban age discrimination by employers and includes provisions aimed at extending the rights of disabled people. However, it stopped short of forcing employers to reveal how much they pay men compared with women, as had been planned by the Labour government.

"By making the law easier to understand, the Equality Act will help businesses treat staff fairly and meet the needs of a diverse customer base," May said. "The law will be easier to understand and better able to protect people from discrimination. A successful economy needs the full participation of all its citizens and we are committed to implementing the Act in the best way for business."

The act was also stripped of "Harriman's Law" that required councils to tackle social deprivation. This "socio-economic duty" had been part of Harriet Harman's Equities Bill and had been described as "socialism in one clause". May argued that it would permanently skew public spending.

"Council services like bin collection and bus routes designed not on the basis of practical need but on this one politically motivated target," she said. "You can't solve a problem as complex as inequality in one legal clause. The idea that they could was symptomatic of Labour's approach to Britain's problems. They thought they could make people's lives better by simply passing a law saying that they should be made better. This was as ridiculous as it was simplistic. And that's why I'm announcing today that we are scrapping Harman's law for good. We shouldn't just compensate people for the barriers to opportunity that they face, we should take action to tear down those barriers altogether."

Otherwise on social policy, she expressed a personal view in 2012 that the legal limit on abortion should be lowered from twenty-four to twenty weeks. Along with most Conservative MPs she voted against an outright ban on foxhunting.

May found herself increasingly fatigued during the summer of 2012. She put this down to her hectic schedule during the London Olympics. Then in November of that year she came down with a heavy cold, with the Home Secretary's first thought that she should get it checked out by her GP. Her husband had just had a similar cold that had developed into bronchitis, so she thought she should get it checked out by her GP.

During the consultation, she mentioned that she had lost a lot of weight recently, though she had put it down to all the dashing about she did as Home Secretary. Nevertheless, the GP did a blood test and discovered she had diabetes. It was only then that she realised she had all the classic symptoms. As long with weight loss, she was drinking more water than usual and making frequent trips to the loo.

Initially she was diagnosed with Type 2 diabetes, which usually occurs after the age of forty. It can be control by diet and tablets. But when the medication didn't work, further tests showed she had Type 1, or insulin-dependent diabetes.

"My very first reaction was that it's impossible because at my age you don't get it," she told *Balance*, the magazine of Diabetes UK. "Then my reaction was: 'Oh no, I'm going to have to inject' and thinking about what that would mean in practical terms."

Colleagues were shocked. One said: "She was someone who never got ill, so she was quite upset because it made her feel vulnerable." But this was rapidly replaced by her customary pragmatism.

The switch in diagnosis meant she had to change from taking tablets to having two insulin injections a day, which later increased to four a day. Although she was familiar with the disease – a cousin had developed it as a teenager – like anyone with diabetes, she found herself on a steep learning curve, discovering what managing it meant in practical terms.

"I hadn't appreciated the degree of management it requires," she said. "I hadn't appreciated, for example, the paradox that while everyone assumes diabetes is about not eating sugar. If you have a hypo, then you have to take something that's got that high glucose content."

Managing the condition while being Home Secretary presented unique challenges.

"The extra issues for me are that I eat out a lot," she explained. "I go to a lot of functions where I am eating and I speak at dinners, so that brings an added complication. When I'm going to do a debate or speaking at a conference, I have to make sure that I've tested and know where I am, so I can adjust as necessary."

Keeping on top of her condition has even led to her surreptitiously breaking the House of Commons' strict rule banning eating in the chamber. There was one occasion when she had to go into the chamber late for an all-night sitting.

"The debates were drawn up meant I had to go in at 11am and I knew I wasn't coming out till about five," she recalled. "I had a bag of nuts in my handbag and one of my colleagues would lean forward every now and then, so that I could eat some nuts without being seen by the speaker."

Despite her high-profile job with its irregular hours, she put herself in the same boat as anyone else with Type 1 diabetes.

"In basic management terms, it's the same for everybody," she said. "You have to get into a routine where you are regularly doing the testing."

Part of her approach to diabetes was being upfront about it.

"I don't inject insulin at the table, but I'm quite open about it," she said. "For example, I was at a dinner last night and needed to inject and so I just said to people: 'You do start eating, I've got to go and do my insulin'. It's better to be open like that."

She said she drew inspiration from Olympic rower Steve Redgrave, a fellow sufferer. When she was first diagnosed, she was very struck by a quote on the Olympian's website where he said that diabetes had to learn to live with him, rather than him living with diabetes.

"I think that's a very good way of looking at it," she said. "Somebody did say to me that they were very surprised I've got diabetes because I don't lead a 'dissolute lifestyle'. And, of course, I said: 'I've got Type 1 – it's an autoimmune condition'. But, the reaction from people with diabetes is that it's good that somebody's come out and said they have diabetes."

In July 2013, she told the *Mail on Sunday* about her condition, which carries an increased risk of heart attacks and stroke.

"It was a real shock and, yes, it took me a while to come to terms with it," she said.

She admitted carrying a needle at all times and had to inject herself regularly during her eighteen-hour days.

"The diabetes doesn't affect how I do the job or what I do. It's just part of life... so it's a case of head down and getting on with it," she told the newspaper.

She regularly worked on ministerial papers until 1 am, starting again a 6.

"It doesn't and will not affect my ability to do my work," she said. "I'm a little more careful about what I eat and there's obviously the injections, but this is something of millions of people have... I'm okay with needles, fortunately."

When she had at first lost weight, there had been rumours that she had been slimming down in order to take on David Cameron.

"This was no some great Machiavellian plan," she insisted. "There was no leadership bid."

The loss of weight had been noted by Allison Pearson of the *Daily Telegraph* though, as usual, it was overshadowed by comments about May's outfits. Pearson remarked: "On the day we meet, the tips of those hands are coated in vermilion. Curiously, while incredibly buttoned up, Mrs May is one of the few flamboyantly stylish women in Westminster. She has lost a lot of weight since becoming Home Secretary (pressure of work, a flu bug that lasted two months, thrice weekly visits to the gym). She is tall and almost too slender in a brown-flecked bouclé jacket worn over a pencil skirt that reveals the best pair of pins in parliament. They are parked in those trademark kitten heels. It's as though the clothes and shoes are allowed to speak while the politician within must remain neutral."

Her tiredness was put down to the fact that her last two summer holidays had been cut short – first by the riots, then when two policemen, Nicola Hughes and Fiona Bone, were shot dead in Manchester. Their killer, Dale Cregan, was sentence to life with no possibility of parole.

For someone who had always kept her private life separate from her career, having such an intense scrutiny of her personal circumstances was not something Theresa May relished.

"I suppose it wasn't that easy because I'm not somebody throughout my political career who's talked much about their personal life," she said. "I've always tended to rely on it being about the policies and politics and so forth, and so it was quite a decision to come out and say it in that way. But, the reaction overall has been pretty positive. I've been interested in the number of people, particularly in the six months after it became public, who came up to me at events and talked about being diabetic and I still will get people who come up and talk to me about it."

After her condition was made public, May was interviewed about it on BBC Radio 5 live and lent her support to charity work. She wrote to schools in her Maidenhead constituency about Diabetes UK's campaign to make sure schools understand the support they are legally required to give children with Type 1 diabetes. Above all, she said she hoped that by doing the demanding role of Home Secretary, she could play a part in dispelling the myth that having diabetes holds people back as she did let her diabetes have any impact on her schedule or her hobbies.

"I would like the message to get across that it doesn't change what you can do," she explained. "The more people can see that people with diabetes can lead a normal life doing the sort of things that other people do, the easier it is for those who are diagnosed with it to deal with it. The fact is that you can still do whatever you want to do, for example, on holiday my husband and I do a lot of quite strenuous walking up mountains in Switzerland, and it doesn't stop me doing it. I can still do things like that and can still do the job. But, people who don't understand it assume that the fact you have a condition means there must be something you can't do; that it must change how you live your life in some way. And, of course, it does change your life in that you have to make sure you've got the right diet and that you're managing your blood sugar levels, but, beyond making sure you've got that routine, you just get on with other things exactly the same."

Along with Alpine walking her other passion was cooking. Despite her busy life, she refused to buy her groceries on line as she enjoyed pushing a trolley through Twyford Waitrose in her Berkshire constituency. She had over a hundred cookbooks and liked to try a new recipe every week. Asked whether she was a Mary Berry or a Delia person at Christmas and she explodes: "Not Delia! I will not allow a Delia Smith cookbook in my house! It's all so precise with Delia, and it makes cooking seem so inaccessible. With somebody like Jamie Oliver, you don't actually have to worry if you've got one little bit of bicarb wrong."

She was a fan of *Masterchef* and had never watched *Game of Thrones*, which was Michael Gove's fare.

Chapter Eight – May the Force Be With You

On 7 July 2013, May had a notable success in a deportation case when she sent radical cleric Abu Qatada back to his native Jordan. He had been arrested under anti-terrorism laws in 2001. Though he was never prosecuted in the UK, he had been convicted in absentia on terrorism charges in Jordan. However, British judges found the case against him had relied on evidence extracted under torture and barred his deportation. Previous Home Secretaries had been unable to remove him, spending £1.7 million in legal fees in the attempt.

After the British court vacillated over his detention, the European Court of Human Rights ruled that Abu Qatada could not be deported to Jordan as that would be a violation of his right to a fair trial under Article 6 of the European Convention on Human Rights. It would also have been illegal under the UN Convention Against Torture.

May took the bull by the horns, met with representatives of the Jordanian government and secured three key assurances. Evidence obtained under torture could not be used against him in any re-trial. His case would be heard by a civilian jury rather than a military panel and that his co-defendants were to be released with a pardon.

"The assurances and information the government has secured from Jordan mean we can undertake deportation in full compliance with the law and with the ruling of the European Court of Human Rights," she said.

The European Court of Human Rights agreed and refused Abu Qatada the right to appeal the latest deportation order. However, Britain's Special Immigration Appeals Commission ruled against the Home Secretary. Their decision was upheld by the Court of Appeal, who denied her leave to appeal. But in May 2013, Abu Qatada agreed to leave provided the UK and Jordanian governments ratified the treaty that evidence gained through torture would not be used against him in any forthcoming trial. That done, he was flown to Jordan.

Meanwhile May vowed to deal with the "crazy interpretation of our human rights laws", including possibly withdrawing from the European Convention of Human Rights. She blamed the European Court of Human Rights in Strasbourg, insisting that the radical Islamist cleric would have been sent back to Jordan long before had it not "moved the goalposts". And she was praised by MPs of all parties.

The following year, Abu Qatada was found not guilty by the Jordanian courts and released, but May asserted that he would not be allowed back into Britain.

May went on to ban khat, an African plant whose leaves are chewed for its stimulant effect. This was done against the advice of the Advisory Committee on the Misuse of Drug, who found there was no risk of harm to most uses. She banned it on the ground that it was outlawed in most EU countries and the United States. It put her at odds with Lib Dem Norman Baker, Minister of State at the Home

Office, who accused her of stripping proposals to liberalise drug laws from a report. This led to his resignation.

In August 2013, May backed the Metropolitan Police when they detained David Miranda for nine hours at Heathrow Airport under the Terrorism Act. Miranda was the partner of *Guardian* columnist Glenn Greenwald, who published a series of articles based on NSA documents leaked by American whistle-blower Edward Snowden, the former CIA employee who had sought asylum in Russia.

Miranda was on his way from Berlin to his home in Brazil. He was found to be carrying an external hard drive, which was seized. The data on it was encrypted using a system called TrueCrypt. Detective Superintendent Caroline Goode, heading the case, said that this rendered the material extremely difficult to access. The hard drive contained around sixty gigabytes of data and only twenty gigabytes had been unscrambled. She said that she had been advised that the hard drive contains "approximately 58,000 UK documents which are highly classified in nature, to the highest level". Goode said the process to decode the material was complex and that "so far only seventy-five documents have been reconstructed since the property was initially received".

A tip-off had come from the White House and May had been given prior notice of the Met's intentions. Deputy Prime Minister Nick Clegg had not been informed and was one of many who thought that Schedule 7 of the Act, which gives the police powers to stop and search anyone they suspect was involved with terrorism, had been misused in the Miranda case.

May was robust in her defence of the police, saying: "If it is believed that somebody has in their possession highly sensitive stolen information which could help terrorists, which could lead to a loss of lives, then it is right that the police act and that is what the law enables them to do."

The Home Office added: "Those who oppose this sort of action need to think about what they are condoning."

Former Director of Public Prosecutions Lord Macdonald then rounded on May.

"That is a rather ugly argument," he said. "To suggest that people who are concerned about the use of a power of this sort against journalists are condoning terrorism, which seems to be the implication of that remark, is an extremely ugly and unhelpful sentiment. People who are concerned about these issues are not condoning terrorism. They are asking a perfectly legitimate question, which is: are we striking the balance in the right place between security and liberty?"

He added: "Let's wait and see what the independent review of this episode has to say before we start accusing people of condoning terrorism and nonsense of that sort."

Shadow Home Secretary Yvette Cooper demanded that May investigate, while the Chairman of the Home Affairs Committee Keith Vaz wrote to the Commissioner of the Metropolitan Police for an explanation. The matter went to the high court where three judges ruled that, while seizing the hard drive was "an indirect interference with press freedom", it was justified by legitimate interests of national security and Miranda's detention was lawful, proportionate and did not breach European human rights protections of freedom of expression.

"In my judgment, the Schedule 7 stop was a proportionate measure in the circumstances," said Mr Justice Law. "Its objective was not only legitimate but very pressing."

May took on the courts again when she stripped Iraqi-born Hilal Al-Jedda of his British citizenship for the second time. He had fled Saddam Hussein's regime in 1992 and claimed asylum in the UK. Under Iraqi law at the time, he automatically lost his nationality when he became a British citizen in 2000. In 2004, he was captured by US forces in Iraq and transferred him to UK custody where he was held without charge for three years. Before he was released, he was stripped of his UK citizenship, but launched a series of appeals. In 2013, the Supreme Court ruled that this was illegal as it left him stateless. Nevertheless, May issued a second "deprivation order", on the grounds that the new Iraqi government recognised him as a citizen. Al-Jedda was living in Turkey at the time. She added a clause to the Immigration Bill, allowing the Home Secretary to remove the citizenship of certain individuals, even if it left them stateless.

She took a similarly hard line in the case of Nigerian asylum-seeker Isa Muazu, who claimed to be fleeing death threats by the Islamist group Boko Haram. He was diagnosed as psychotic and suffering from severe depression. While in detention at Harmondsworth Immigration Removal Centre, he went on a hunger strike which lasted three months. When medical staff informed the Home Office that Muazu was not fit to be detained because of his deteriorating medical condition, they issued an "end of life plan". A private jet was hired to fly him back to Nigeria, despite fears that he might not survive the flight, and Lib Dem peer Lord Roberts of Llandudno accused May of "allowing people to die to score a political point".

The following year, May was embroiled in further furore when there were delays in the issuing of passports. This was due to the cutbacks and closed processing facilities overseas. It turned out that May had been warned of this a year earlier. Bonuses were paid to staff to work longer hours to clear the backlog.

She had long had an enemy with the Police Federation since she had first started talking about cuts and reform when she came to office in 2010. Two years later, she had been forced to take the stage at their conference in front of a banner saying "cutting police by 20 per cent is criminal". An estimated 1,200 delegates stood up and brandished signs reading "enough is enough" and her speech was received in silence when she told them: "Let's stop pretending the police are being picked on. Every part of the public sector is having to take its share of the pain."

There were cheers in the question-and-answer session when one delegate said: "I believe you are a disgrace."

The final speaker in 2012 told her: "Home Secretary you may not like this but we no longer trust you in the police service." And as the

Home Secretary left the stage there were boos and shouts of "resign".

In May 2014, she got her own back, beginning her speech by detailing their faults.

"In the last few years, we have seen the Leveson Inquiry…"

As well as dealing with phone hacking, Leveson looked into corrupt relationships between the press and police."

"…The appalling conclusions of the Hillsborough independent panel…"

It found that 116 of the 164 police statements had been amended in a cover-up which sought to deflect responsibility for the disaster from the police onto Liverpool fans.

"…The death of Ian Tomlinson and the sacking of PC Harwood.…"

Tomlinson was the newspaper vendor who died after being struck by a police officer during the 2009 G-20 summit protests in the City of London. PC Simon Harwood was found not guilty of manslaughter, but was dismissed from the Metropolitan Police for gross misconduct.

"…The ongoing inquiry by an independent panel into the murder of Daniel Morgan.…"

Private investigator David Morgan had been murdered while allegedly investigating police corruption. The case against those thought to be responsible collapsed, though one of the defendants served time for perverting the course of justice, before taking centre stage during the phone-hacking scandal for providing confidential information from a network of corrupt policeman.

"...The first sacking of a chief constable for gross misconduct in modern times...."

Cleveland Police chief Sean Price was sacked after it was found he lied to the Independent Police Complaints Commission about helping the police authority chairman's daughter get a job with the force and told others to do the same.

"...The investigation of more than ten senior officers for acts of alleged misconduct and corruption. Allegations of rigged recorded crime statistics. The sacking of PCs Keith Wallis, James Glanville and Gillian Weatherley after 'Plebgate'. Worrying reports by the inspectorate about stop and search and domestic violence. The Herne Review into the conduct of the Metropolitan Police Special Demonstration Squad. The Ellison Review into allegations of corruption during the investigation of the murder of Stephen Lawrence. Further allegations that the police sought to smear Stephen's family..."

May then went for the jugular.

"When you remember the list of recent revelations about police misconduct, it is not enough to mouth platitudes about 'a few bad apples'," she said. "The problem might lie with a minority of officers, but it is still a significant problem, and a problem that needs to be addressed.... It cannot be right when officers under investigation by the IPCC comply with the rules by turning up for interview but then refuse to co-operate and decline to answer questions. Such behaviour – which I am told is often encouraged by the Federation – reveals an attitude that is far removed from the principles of public service felt by the majority of police officers."

She went on to address a case when officers called to help a woman who had suffered domestic violence accidentally recorded themselves calling the victim a "slag" and a "bitch".

"It is the same attitude expressed when young black men ask the police why they are being stopped and searched and are told it is 'just routine' even though according to the law, officers need 'reasonable grounds for suspicion'. It is an attitude that betrays contempt for the public these officers are supposed to serve – and every police officer in the land, every single police leader, and everybody in the Police Federation should confront it and expunge it from the ranks."

The police were told, in no uncertain terms, to change or they would be changed.

"According to one survey carried out recently, only 42 per cent of black people from a Caribbean background trust the police. That is simply not sustainable.... I will soon publish proposals to strengthen the protections available to whistle-blowers in the police. I am creating a new criminal offence of police corruption. And I am determined that the use of stop and search must come down, become more targeted and lead to more arrests."

The Federation itself had to change too as a review had found a lack of transparency and openness in its affairs and finances, and there had been allegations of bullying and victimisation. The review's thirty-six recommendations were to be implement. Meanwhile she was cutting off the Federation's funding.

The delegates were left in a state of "shock and bewilderment," according to one of the candidates to be the Federation's new chairman. Another branded her a bully.

However, with this fortitude, May won the grudging admiration of her opposite number, despite their many disagreements.

"I respect her style – it is steady and serious. She is authoritative in parliament – superficial attacks on her bounce off," Yvette Cooper told the *Guardian*. "The flip side is that she is not fleet of foot when crises build, she digs in her heels – remember the Passport Agency crisis in 2014 when the backlog caused hundreds to miss their holidays, and the Border Force crisis in 2011 when border checks were axed.

"And she hides when things go wrong. No interviews, no quotes, nothing to reassure people or to remind people she even exists. It's helped her survive as Home Secretary – but if you are Prime Minister, eventually the buck has to stop."

Chapter Nine – Mayfair

In June 2014 a fresh row erupted between Theresa May and Education Secretary Michael Gove over the supposed Trojan Horse plot in which Islamic extremists allegedly attempted to gain control of schools in Birmingham. A letter from May to Gove concerning the Extremist Task Force's Code of Practice appeared briefly on a government website.

In it May said: "The allegations relating to schools in Birmingham raise serious questions about the quality of school governance and oversight arrangements in the maintained sector, not just the supplementary schools that would be signatories to this Code of Practice. How did it come to pass, for example, that one of the governors at Park View was the chairman of the education committee of the Muslim Council of Britain? Is it true that Birmingham City Council was warned about these allegations in 2008? Is it true that the Department for Education was warned in 2010? If so, why did nobody act? I am aware that several investigations are still ongoing and those investigations are yet to conclude."

It was quickly deleted and David Cameron had to step in between the two warring Cabinet ministers. He insisted that May sack her media adviser Fiona Cunningham over the leak. Cunningham, now Fiona Hill, returned as Downing Street Chief of Staff when May became premier. Meanwhile Gove was forced to apologise for briefing against May's counter-terrorism adviser Charles Farr, who was Ms Cunningham's lover. However, the rift left relations between Number Ten and the Home Office at an all-time low. May took particular flak.

"Her working style and that of her team is very closed, very controlling, very untrusting," said a Tory source at the time. "They don't share. They see conspiracies around every corner and think everyone is either briefing against or undermining them, so they brief first. That's their operating style… it's just a pain in the arse."

Yet May won more grudging respect for her refusal to play the game.

"There is a steeliness to her which is impressive," continued the source. "One of the things I admire about her is that you know you don't mess with her. David Cameron knows it's a minister who is going to fight back a bit."

Simon Danczuk, the Labour MP for Rochdale, who has been instrumental in setting up the Westminster child abuse inquiry which is overseen by May, said she was "an extremely professional, smart woman. She's very clever and she really listens to what people have to say."

However, there was a downside. "She comes across as quite cold, whereas David Cameron – for all his faults, you'd go for a drink with him," he added.

Indeed, according to her former campaign manager Sam Olsen, she was hardly convivial.

"She likes to drink a St Clements," he said. That's orange juice mixed with lemonade. "And she never swears."

According to a Conservative backbencher, May was fundamentally unknowable, not given to small-talk or easily shared confidences. She could be aloof and difficult to get close to, which was then thought of as an obstacle to any potential leadership bid. She was also compared to Karla, the inscrutable Soviet spymaster in John le Carré's novels.

"She's sphinx-like," said the backbencher. "I played a game with her once, which was trying to out-silence her in a meeting. She'll give nothing away. She'll sit there in silence. It's a good technique, used by interrogators, but I don't think it gets you very far. You don't feel you're having a conversation."

Others point out that her apparent distance was the result of an innate shyness and caution. She was a private person in an over-sharing age.

"I suppose I'm not naturally over-effusive in wanting to go out there and tell everybody my story," May said in an interview with *Total Politics* magazine. "Showing that you can do something, that you're in the job and doing it, is more important than the back-story."

A colleague said: "If you were to ask me for an anecdote, I'd find it hard to think of one. Except that she can be a bit annoying."

Another colleague rose to the challenge, saying: "She stores her shoes in see through plastic boxes."

However, she did exhibit a softer side when she was relaxed. Olsen recalled her being warm and kind to his toddler son, Lawrence.

"He was crawling around her house, pulling out books, and she didn't care," he said.

At dinner parties, she often made a beeline for other women and seemed genuinely interested in their lives. If one of her closer team of advisers was ill or had personal difficulties, May would stay in touch with regular phone calls and texts.

"She is like a tigress looking after her litter," said one. "That's nice to know and it makes you want to work harder... She respects competence. She respects when people are willing to work hard – not just talking the talk, but walking the walk... She's got exacting standards, don't get me wrong. Unless you have those standards, maybe you find it hard working for her."

Once she got so frustrated by a civil servant's inability to answer a direct question, she banged her head on the table. On another occasion, she was said to have physically taken an official from Number Ten by the lapels of his jacket and removed him from the Home Office. Dedicated to the job, she was sometimes still poring over her red boxes at 2 am and had been known to reply to emails on Christmas Eve.

Though the job had obviously taken its toll. After she had served as Home Secretary for four years in the job, an MP noted: "She came across as almost fragile. She's quite a delicate woman. She's tall, her shoulders were sort of rounded. She was probably feeling a bit frazzled".

This was put down to determination to be on top of her brief.

"She's such a details person, she does actually read every submission back to front," said a former colleague. "Nothing slips through. I've had civil servants say, 'She knows more than I do.'"

However, critics insisted she is more of a proficient corporate manager than a creative thinker or an intellectual innovator. She was, they say, simply not very exciting.

"If she does have a broader vision," said a Tory source, "I don't know what it is."

Nevertheless, in November 2014, May was award the ultimate accolade in British life – an appearance on BBC Radio Four's *Desert Island Discs*, where she happily unburdened herself and her choice of music showed a remarkable breadth of taste. Her eight records were:

1. "Walk Like A Man" from the original Broadway production of Jersey Boys.

2. The Gregorian chant "*Pange Lingua Gloriosi Corporis Mysterium*" written by St Thomas Aquinas in the 13th century for the Feast of Corpus.

3. Edward Elgar's Cello Concerto.

4. Abba's "Dancing Queen".

5. The Rondo from the "Abdelazer Suite" by the English Baroque composer Henry Purcell.

6. The "Queen of the Night" aria from Mozart's opera *Magic Flute*.

7. An episode of the BBC TV political satire *Yes Minister* called "The Compassionate Society" from 1981, where minister Jim Hacker is shocked that a new NHS hospital that had been open for fifteen months had yet to admit any patients despite having more than five hundred administrative staff.

8. "When I Survey The Wondrous Cross", a hymn which was written by Isaac Watts, first published in 1707 and used by the BBC to introduce its early morning broadcasts on Good Friday.

Her book was *Pride And Prejudice* by Jane Austen and her luxury item was a lifetime subscription to *Vogue* magazine.

Chapter Ten – May Day

After being re-elected in the 2015 general election with an increased majority, Theresa May had re-appointed Home Secretary, becoming the longest serving Home Secretary since James Chuter Ede, who served in that role in Clement Atlee's Labour government from 1945 to 1951.

At the party conference that October, she devoted her entire speech to the single subject of immigration, beginning by talking about the 1.7 million refugees who had fled the war in Syria. While they were people deserving of help, she said, that help should take the form of aid dispensed to those who stayed in refugee camps in Jordan, Lebanon and Turkey, not to those who have fled to Europe. She defended the government's decision to accept no more than five thousand Syrian refugees a year, and criticised Angela Merkel for deciding that Germany would take in 800,000 refugees. This, she believed, was an inducement for people from all over the world to try to get into Germany.

Now that the Conservatives had a majority, May announced that she would introduce a new Draft Communications Data Bill, earlier denounced as a Snooper's Charter when the Lib Dems had blocked it in coalition. This would become the Draft Investigatory Powers Bill after some of the more contentious clauses had been dropped.

"For example we won't be requiring communication service providers from in the UK to store third-party data, we won't be making the same requirements in relation to data retention on overseas CSPs," May told Andrew Marr. "And crucially, we will not be giving powers to go through people's browsing history. That is not what the investigatory powers bill is about."

She said she would set out strong oversight and authorisation arrangements for warrants to access more intrusive data. More than 1,400 warrants authorising more intrusive measures crossed the Home Secretary's desk a year. She had to set aside several hours a day to consider them and wanted this responsibility to be handed over to judges.

There were other concerns.

"Encryption is important for people to be able to keep themselves safe when they are dealing with these modern communications in the digital age but we will be setting out the current position, which does enable the authorities with proper authorisation to issue warrants," she said.

Although May supported the UK remaining in the EU during the 2016 referendum campaign, on the stump she exhibited a fair degree of Euroscepticism, noting particularly that freedom of movement under EU rules prevented her getting net immigration down. In fact, she took little part in the debate, going about her usual business as Home Secretary. In the middle of the campaign, she announced an official review of the application of sharia law in England and Wales as part of the government's country-extremism strategy.

"Many British people of different faiths follow religious codes and practices, and benefit a great deal from the guidance they offer," she said. However, the review would look into the extent sharia law was being misused or applied in a way that was incompatible with the rule of law in Britain. It would also assess ways in which sharia law may be causing harm in communities.

"A number of women have reportedly been victims of what appear to be discriminatory decisions taken by sharia councils, and that is a significant concern," she said. "There is only one rule of law in our country, which provides rights and security for every citizen."

May had raised the prospect of such an inquiry in March 2015, saying there was evidence of women being "divorced" under sharia law and left in penury. She also said wives were being forced to return to abusive relationships because sharia councils said a husband had a right to "chastise" them, and that sharia councils gave the testimony of a woman only half the weight of that of a man.

Casting herself as a reluctant Remainer, she said that Britain needed to leave the European Convention on Human Rights, later saying that she would not pursue this due to lack of parliamentary support. And she asked whether it was "really right" for the EU to give countries like Turkey "all the rights of membership". One observer called her "the chief Eurosceptic for In".

"She's in a strategically good position, but that is just a by-product of the type of politician she is," said one Tory minister. "It's just part of her nature – all this shouting across the aisles is anathema to her."

It was said that she gave the impression of being a sensible woman, getting on with her job while the public schoolboys squabbled over Europe. Just a week before referendum day, she said that, in his renegotiation, David Cameron had not done enough to satisfy public concerns on immigration. She also made it clear that Brexit did not worry her, writing: "We are the fifth biggest economy in the world and obviously big enough and strong enough to survive in or out of the EU."

There was criticism of her lukewarm support. One pro-Remain minister said: "Theresa is hiding in the hope there will be no blood on her at the end of all this." Even before the country had voted for Brexit, there was speculation that she was already lining herself for a leadership bid. During the referendum campaign, David Cameron said that he would not stand down if he lost. However, in the run up to the 2015 general election he had announced that he would not run for a third term, so it was clear that there would be a vacancy within the parliament.

However, he took everyone by surprise on the morning of 24 June 2016, the day after the referendum, when he announced that, having lost the campaign to remain in the EU, he was standing down, though he would stay in post until a new leader of the Conservative Party was elected. The new Prime Minister should be in office by the party conference in October, he said. But this plan was quickly overtaken by events.

As the country had voted to leave the EU, it was thought that Boris Johnson, backed by his ally in the Leave campaign Michael Gove, was in line for the top job. They had already hired Lynton Crosby, the Australian political strategist who had masterminded Boris successful campaign for London mayor in 2008. However, it soon became clear that Theresa May, though a tactic Remainer, had support as a unity candidate.

On the Tuesday before nominations opened, Johnson had the support of around a hundred MPs, while May had seventy to eighty. However, opinion polls put May ahead among both Tory voters and the public generally. Soon she was the bookmaker's favourite.

May announced her candidacy on 30 June wearing, it was remarked, a Vivian Westwood tartan trouser suit. Despite being a Remainer, she reassured the electorate that there would be no going back on the outcome of the referendum.

"The campaign was fought, the vote was held, turnout was high and the public gave their verdict," she said. "There must be no attempts to remain inside the EU, no attempts to rejoin it through the back door and no second referendum… Brexit means Brexit."

There would be no early election, no emergency budget and Article 50 of the Lisbon Treaty, formally invoking exit from the EU, should not be trigger until the end of 2016 at the earliest.

She concluded her short speech, outlining her qualifications for the job.

"As Home Secretary, I was told I couldn't take on the Police Federation, but I did. I was told I couldn't cut police spending without crime going up, but crime is lower than ever. I was told I shouldn't start asking questions about police corruption, but everywhere I've seen it – from Stephen Lawrence to Hillsborough – I've exposed it. I was told I couldn't stop Gary McKinnon's extradition, but I stood up to the American Government and I stopped it. I was told I couldn't deport Abu Qatada, but I flew to Jordan and negotiated the treaty that got him out of Britain for good."

In the following question and answer session, she dismissed Johnson's negotiating skills: "The last time he did a deal with the Germans he came back with three nearly new water cannon."

She dismissed a suggestion from a journalist that she bore similarities to German Chancellor Angela Merkel, saying: "I know I'm not a showy politician. I don't tour the television studios. I don't gossip about people over lunch. I don't go drinking in parliament's bars. I don't often wear my heart on my sleeve. I just get on with the job in front of me."

She also had local backing. Glenn Mitchell, deputy editor of the *Maidenhead Advertiser*, described her as a "hardworking constituency MP". He said: "She has always managed to balance her responsibilities in Maidenhead and Tywford with other duties as a leading Conservative figure. She is also extremely popular, reflected in the fact she has been an MP for more than a decade and polled nearly 60 per cent of the constituency vote in the recent general election."

She had barely finished speaking when the campaign was thrown into chaos. Michael Gove turned against Boris Johnson and announced that he would run for the leadership in a move seen as a stab in the back. Johnson then announced that, against all expectations, he would not be running. That left five candidates – May, Gove, Secretary of State for Work and Pensions Stephen Crabb, former Minister of Defence Liam Fox and Minster of State for Energy Andrea Leadsom, a leading Leaver now endorsed by Boris Johnson.

Under the rules for electing a new leader, a series of ballots are held by the parliamentary party, with the candidate winning the fewest votes eliminated each time. When there are only two candidates left, their names are put to the full membership of the party, who make the final decision in a postal ballot.

The first ballot of MPs was held on 5 July. May came first. Fox came fifth and was knocked out, while Crabb withdrew. Both then endorsed Gove. In the next ballot, May again was the clear winner and Gove was knocked out, so May and Leadsom's names would be put to the party in the country.

On 11 July, May began her national campaign with a speech in Birmingham, saying she had the overwhelming support of her colleagues in the House of Commons.

"Nearly two thirds of the Conservative Party in Parliament. Left and right. Leavers and Remainers. MPs from the length and breadth of Britain."

She called for more house building and a proper industrial strategy. And she said that she wanted to crack down on the excesses of big business, including executive and putting workers' representatives on the board.

"I want to see changes in the way that big business is governed. The people who run big businesses are supposed to be accountable to outsiders," she said. "In practice, they are drawn from the same narrow social and professional circles as the executive team."

While May was travelling back to London after the speech, news broke that Leadsom had withdrawn from the contest following some tactless remarks about being better to lead the country because she had children. As the sole remaining candidate, May was confirmed as leader of the Conservative Party that evening.

Chapter Eleven – Maggie May?

At one final cabinet meeting the following, tributes to the departing Prime Minister were led by Theresa May and George Osborne, who had flown back from America to attend. David Cameron then said that May was the right person to lead the country forward wisely. Afterwards she stayed behind with him for half-an-hour. May again made it clear that there would be no early election and her government would run until 2020. Labour had called for a snap election, but that was no longer a simple matter after the Fixed-Term Parliament Act of 2011. Meanwhile a blue removals van arrived in Downing Street.

This was a matter of urgency as Theresa May and her husband planned to live in the flat above Number Eleven, where the Camerons had installed a £25,000 luxury kitchen after they arrived in Downing Street in 2010. Osborne's smaller family had lived in the flat above Number Ten. Cameron had treated May to a tour. However, according to *MailOnline*, Theresa May planned a renovation of the minimalist stainless-steel kitchen, abandoning the Italian theme. The website warned her that, post-Brexit, the price of new kitchen appliances was set to soar.

The luxury kitchen was used one last time the evening before the Camerons moved out. Busy moving, they had a takeaway curry delivered from Kennington Tandoori.

The Mays also favoured curry. According to the *Daily* their favourite restaurant was an upmarket Indian called Malik's in Cookham, but they rarely went there as she preferred cooking at home.

That night though, Theresa and Philip had dinner with the Chief Rabbi Ephraim Mirvis in his north London home. He described Mrs May as "a friend and champion of our community and of other faiths".

In a statement issued the following morning: "I recall the speed and the sensitivity with which she reached out to the Jewish community following the terror attacks on Jewish targets in Europe last year. As she made clear then, 'Without its Jews, Britain would not be Britain.' She has proved herself to be a friend and champion of our community and of other faith communities who share her values of tolerance and understanding. Last night, on the eve of her becoming Prime Minister, Theresa May kept a long-standing arrangement to join Valerie and me at our home for dinner. The fact that she did this in the midst of critically important preparations before taking up office is a reflection of her strong desire to keep to her commitments and the esteem in which she holds the British Jewish community."

On 13 July, David Cameron took a last session of Prime Minister's questions with Theresa May sitting beside him. In the house, he warmly congratulated her and told leader of the opposition Jeremy Corbyn: "When it comes to female Prime Ministers, I am pleased to say pretty soon it is going to be two–nil."

After that Cameron went to Buckingham Palace to tender his resignation to the Queen. That afternoon, Theresa May, accompanied by husband, also went to the Palace where she was asked to form a new government. At fifty-nine, she would be the oldest leader to enter Downing Street since James Callaghan in 1976 and was the first Prime Minister since Ted Heath not to have children.

Returning from the Palace, May addressed the press in Downing Street, heaping fulsome praise on Cameron and his government, while signally a clear change of direction.

"The government I lead will be driven not by the interests of the privileged few but by yours," she said. "We will do everything we can to give you more control over your lives. When we take the big calls, we'll think not of the powerful, but you. When we pass new laws we'll listen not to the mighty, but to you. When it comes to taxes we'll prioritise not the wealthy but you."

She spoke of the precious bond between England, Scotland, Wales and Northern Ireland, and between "all of our citizens, every one of us, whoever we are and wherever we're from".

She pledged to continue Cameron's one-nation government.

"That means fighting against the burning injustice that, if you're born poor, you will die on average nine years earlier than others. If you're black, you're treated more harshly by the criminal justice system than if you're white. If you're a white, working-class boy, you're less likely than anybody else in Britain to go to university. If you're at a state school, you're less likely to reach the top professions than if you're educated privately. If you're a woman, you will earn less than a man. If you suffer from mental health problems, there's not enough help to hand. If you're young, you'll find it harder than ever before to own your own home.

"But the mission to make Britain a country that works for everyone means more than fighting these injustices. If you're from an ordinary working class family, life is much harder than many people in Westminster realise. You have a job but you don't always have job security. You have your own home, but you worry about paying a mortgage. You can just about manage but you worry about the cost of living and getting your kids into a good school."

Again she committed herself to Brexit.

"We are living through an important moment in our country's history," she said. "Following the referendum, we face a time of great national change. And I know because we're Great Britain, that we will rise to the challenge. As we leave the European Union, we will forge a bold new positive role for ourselves in the world, and we will make Britain a country that works not for a privileged few, but for every one of us. That will be the mission of the government I lead, and together we will build a better Britain."

Theresa May then began a brutal cull of the cabinet. Nine ministers were sacked or resigned. George Osborne was ousted within hours of her taking office, to be replaced by former Foreign Secretary Philip Hammond. He confirmed that there would be no emergency budget. Osborne's departure was followed by Justice Secretary Michael Gove, Culture Secretary John Whittingdale, Education

Secretary Nicky Morgan, and Chancellor of the Duchy of Lancaster Oliver Letwin.

In a surprise move, Boris Johnson was made foreign secretary. However, some of the post's overseas duties would be taken by lead Brexit campaigner David Davis as Secretary of State for Exiting the European Union and Liam Fox as Secretary of State for International Trade. May also promoted more women. Amber Rudd followed May into the Home Office, while Justine Greening took over as Education Secretary, Andrea Leadsom became Environment Secretary and Liz Truss became Justice Secretary, making her the first female Lord Chancellor in the thousand-year history of the role. May's old friend Damian Green became Secretary of State for Work and Pensions.

Despite May's commitment to Brexit, eighteen of her ministers had supported Remain, while only seven had declared for Leave. However, leading Leavers were in key Brexit negotiating positions so if it went horribly wrong they would shoulder the blame. ITV's Political Editor Robert Peston also noted: "Her rhetoric is more left-wing than Cameron's was, her cabinet is more right wing than his was."

Summing up the change, the *Guardian* said: "In a political party that struggles to shake off its elitist, old Etonian, yah-boo-sucks reputation, May represents a different kind of politician: a calm headmistress in a chamber full of over-excitable public schoolboys. She holds herself at one remove… her obdurate stance has earned her some vociferous critics. There are those who claim that, while she takes care never to sully her own hands with the grubby business of political backstabbing, she will send out her team to issue ferocious briefings against her rivals."

Former Conservative chancellor Ken Clarke, who also had run-ins with May, was recorded on camera ahead of an interview saying that she was good at her job but a "bloody difficult woman" – before adding, as an aside, that so was Mrs Thatcher. In the Conservative Party, this was generally viewed as an endorsement.

The BBC added that Mrs May has never been one of the most clubbable of politicians and was someone who preferred not having to tour the tea rooms of the House of Commons, where tittle-tattle was freely exchanged.

Unlike Tony Blair or David Cameron, she did not schmooze.

"She doesn't flirt," said a male Conservative MP. "She doesn't use sex as a weapon. Thatcher did, by all accounts. Theresa is almost asexual. I think we're dealing with a mature, wise, experienced and competent politician but what she lacks, I think, is warmth and personality on first meeting."

But then she had her rock, her husband Philip, with her in Downing Street.

"He's been at her side for the six years while she's been a busy Home Secretary, so he's well versed in all this – the discipline, the security, the red boxes," said Alan Duncan, the new minister of state at the Foreign Office. "He's very sharp, always steady. It's inconceivable to think of him ever doing anything embarrassing.

On 15 July, May travelled to Scotland to meet first minister Nicola Sturgeon amid rumours that there might be a second referendum on independence as Scotland voted decisively to remain in the EU.

"I believe with all my heart in the United Kingdom – the precious bond between England, Scotland, Wales and Northern Ireland," said May. "This visit to Scotland is my first as Prime Minister and I'm coming here to show my commitment to preserving this special union that has endured for centuries."

Despite Sturgeon's commitment for Scotland to stay in the EU, May said she was unwilling to consider a second referendum on independence as the Scottish people had delivered a "very clear message" in 2014. However, she was "willing to listen to options and I've been very clear with the first minister today that I want the Scottish government to be fully engaged in our discussion. I have already said that I won't be triggering Article 50 until I think that we have a UK approach and objectives for negotiations – I think it is important that we establish that before we trigger Article 50."

But Sturgeon was adamant.

"It would be inconceivable for any Prime Minister to seek to stand in the way of a referendum if that is what the Scottish parliament voted for," she said.

On 18 July, May took her place on the government front bench during the debate on the future of Trident. When asked whether she was you prepared to authorise a nuclear strike that could kill hundreds of thousands of men, women and children, May said: "Yes. And I have to say to the honourable gentleman the whole point of a deterrent is that our enemies need to know that we would be prepared to use it, unlike some suggestions that we could have a deterrent but not actually be willing to use it, which seem to come from the Labour party frontbench."

Two days later, she made her debut at Prime Minister's questions. With her husband waving from the peers' gallery, she made a devastating attack on Jeremy Corbyn.

"In my years here in this house I've long heard the Labour party asking what the Conservatives party does for women," she said. "It just keeps making us Prime Minister."

She also mentioned that the Conservative Party had also made "a working-class boy from Brixton" – that is, John Major – Prime Minister, a gibe as Corbyn's distinctly middle-class background.

Ridiculing the Labour's attempts to wrest the leadership from Corbyn, she said: "I look forward to the exchanges he and I will have and I hope we will be having those exchanges over the despatch box for many years to come."

Amid wild cheers and jeering from the Tory benches, Corbyn replied lamely: "'I know this is very funny for many Conservative members… But I am not sure there are many Conservative members who have to go to a food bank."

He then asked her about her promised to improve job security and the lives of ordinary workers.

"I'm interested he refers to the situation of some workers who might have some job insecurity and potentially unscrupulous bosses," she said. "I suspect that there are many members on the opposition benches who might be familiar with an unscrupulous boss. A boss who doesn't listen to his workers. A boss who requires some of his workers to double their workload. And maybe even a boss who exploits the rules to further his own career."

She then asked: "Remind him of anybody?"

Corbyn then shifted his attack to job cuts and austerity.

"He calls it austerity. I call it living within our means." Endorsing Thatcherism, she went on: "Sound finance and government running the affairs of the nation in a sound financial way. It stands for honest money, not inflation. It stands for living within our means."

Labour MP Jamie Reed then drew attention to the divisions in the Conservative ranks during the referendum campaign. May was ready for that.

"The honourable gentleman makes a reference to divisions on the Conservative party benches," she said. "I have to say, which is the party that took three weeks to decide which should be their unity candidate? It was the Labour party."

After winning the battle on the home front, she prepared to fly to Germany to meet Chancellor Merkel, then on to Paris to visit French President François Hollande in the first skirmishes in the war to disentangle the UK from the EU.

Acknowledgements

This file is licensed under the Creative Commons Attribution 2.0 Generic license.

Source:

https://en.wikipedia.org/wiki/File:Theresa_May_UK_Home_Office.jpg

If you enjoyed *Taking Charge* check out Endeavour Press's other books here: Endeavour Press - the UK's leading independent publisher of digital books.

For weekly updates on our free and discounted eBooks sign up to our newsletter.

Follow us on Twitter **and** Goodreads.